M000087696

# BETHUNE

Out of the Darkness into the Light
of Freedom

Written By

Evelyn Bethune
Mary's Grandbaby

# Forwards

This book is about the hunger to be free.  It's a love story, it's a dream of owning your own business and controlling your own life while at the same time, a harsh reminder of man's inhumanity to man.  Starting out with nothing but faith in God and hard work against all odds, this book is about pride and dignity, persistence, and finding a way to make life meaningful all wrapped up into one.  Thus, it is with great honor that I write this forward for my good friend and unstoppable spirit, Dr. Evelyn Bethune, speaker, author, educator, community activist, and servant leader.

Get ready to step back a moment in time so dark that James Weldon Johnson would have called it, "When hope unborn had died." A time when a black enslaved family driven by an unquenchable thirst to be free, inspired by memories of living a life of royalty, and fortified by faith, carved out a tunnel of hope through mountains of despair.  Each page of **BETHUNE: Out of the Darkness into the light of Freedom,** gives us a rare insight into the mindset of a people who refused to be broken all the while experiencing the worst form of slavery and oppression the world has ever known.  Each chapter reminds us just how powerful we are as a people especially when we take into account that during this period black slaves were relegated to being treated like cattle, less than human.

Blacks were lynched if they were caught trying to learn how to read. It was law that a black man had no rights a white man had to respect. Even the great black scientist, George Washington Carver, was traded for a horse when he was a baby. These societal conditions gave birth to the Bethune family.

In spite of such adverse circumstances, however, Patsy McLeod had a child that people in the neighborhood called an old soul, one who was different from all the other children. Her name was Mary McLeod Bethune. Mary always had a passion to educate black people and as an adult, went before the city leaders to ask for help in her quest to establish a school. They grudgingly gave her the city dump to build her school for black children. With a hand full of children including Evelyn's father Albert, they prayed up and summoned up millions of dollars to build an educational institution, which still stands today. Mary went on to become a renowned educator, respected by world leaders and heads of states.

One of her contemporaries, Booker T. Washington, said, "Judge a man not by what he has achieved but by what he had to overcome in order to make his accomplishment." Needless to say, Mary McLeod Bethune and the Bethune family, like most of us, had to overcome a lot. This book written by Mary's granddaughter, Dr. Evelyn Bethune, reveals some of her family's hardships. Many of the things in this book will even shock you. Yet, the Bethune family is still standing, contributing to society, and making their mark in history. **BETHUNE** gives us reason to reflect upon the history of our people with pride while at the same time challenges us to step up and make our voices heard. We are forever indebted to Dr. Evelyn Bethune for sharing and preserving this part of our history and bringing it to our awareness in today's modern times. Thank you, Evelyn, for continuing in the spirit of your grandmother and for making your mark as a BETHUNE.

Les Brown

## The true worth of a race must be measured by the character of its womanhood.
*~Mary McLeod Bethune~*

I met Dr. Evelyn Bethune over the phone in August 2005. I was looking for a family member of Dr. Mary McLeod Bethune to come out to Long Beach Unified School District in California in February 2006 for the dedication of our new state of the art facility devoted to the education of homeless children. The facility and the school district's homeless education plan are named in honor of Dr. Mary McLeod Bethune.

Sometimes when we meet someone for the first time, it feels like we've known each other for a long time. Such is the case with Evelyn Bethune and me. I felt as though I was talking to my own sister. I had been inspired by Dr. Mary McLeod Bethune since I read about her in high school and have read as much as I could about her life since then. Dr. Mary McLeod Bethune has been a "virtual mentor" to me for 30 years and now I was talking to a living relative of hers. I wondered what it must have been like for Evelyn and the other grandchildren growing up in Daytona where everyone knew Mary's story.

My very first impression of Evelyn was, "She is channeling her grandmother." Everything I could expect to hear out of Mary's mouth, I heard from Evelyn's. She is committed to her grandmother's issues of faith, love, equality, the importance of a good education, honoring her heritage, and strong communication about important issues. "The shoes of Mary McLeod Bethune are surely too big to fill," I thought. Evelyn has surrendered to her purpose, and is embracing the great promises of hope her grandmother launched a century ago.

"To whom much is given, much is required." Luke 12:48. Dr. Evelyn Bethune is strong, well-educated, and capable. She is a civil rights leader, an education visionary, and a faithful servant. On February 9, 2006, Dr. Evelyn Bethune spoke on the steps of a new facility built for one purpose, to provide the very best education, medical and psychological help to the very poorest children in the Greater Long Beach California Area. "Thank you," Dr. Bethune began, "For serving the very children who need an education the most. You have taken what you learned from my grandmother and put it into action." Tears rolled down her face when she saw her grandmother's education motto on a banner for homeless children to read everyday. *Enter to learn. Depart to Serve.* "Yet today," she said to the crowd, "my grandmother's message is still relevant."

In Long Beach, California everyone knows about the accomplishments of Dr. Mary McLeod Bethune. The Long Beach Unified School District began educating homeless children in 1991. In Long Beach homeless education is a high priority to everyone from the Board of Education, Superintendent of Schools, Mayor and City

Council, from the Chamber of Commerce to communities of faith, business, nonprofit organizations, public schools, teachers, parents, and the media

Dr. Evelyn Bethune will leave her own legacy on this generation just as her grandmother did in the first half of the twentieth century. Dr. Evelyn Bethune is a woman of her time cherishing the bold initiatives such as equity in education and social services and community development, of her grandmother's but she has made them relevant to our time.

I hope Evelyn's book brings to light to a new generation the impact that her grandmother made on race relations, civil rights, education, community development, personal development, faith, hope, and patience. Indeed, Dr. Martin Luther King, Jr. followed in the footsteps of Dr. Mary McLeod Bethune. Now, however, Dr. Evelyn Bethune is wearing her shoes.

Judy Seal
Executive Director, Long Beach Education Foundation
Long Beach, CA 90810

## To Serwa  a/k/a  Dr. Evelyn Bethune

The Most Honorable Elijah Muhammad teaches that history is best qualified and most attractive to reward our research. Mr. Muhammad observes that a wise person should study ancient and modern history. It is through an intense study of history that one gains insight into their current circumstances and through this process develops the gift of prophecy. By studying the struggle of previous generations, we will be better able to glean the nuggets of wisdom of their experience and chart a course of action needed to overcome all obstacles in our path.

Today, there are opportunities open for some fortunate souls that were not available to those who lived before us. Given our history of slavery and Jim Crow, how is this possible? Conversely, there are doors of opportunity that remain closed to the masses of black people. How do we solve this generational conundrum? With a widening gap between haves and have-nots, what can the black middle class and intelligentsia do to help their suffering people? How do we unite our "talent tenth" with the larger body of working poor? How do we pry open the door of equal opportunity for millions who have not realized the so called American dream?

The importance of this book about Dr. Mary McLeod Bethune's grandchildren and great grandchildren, *BETHUNE: Out of Darkness into the Light of Freedom* cannot be overstated.   My good friend and fellow freedom fighter Dr. Evelyn Bethune, the granddaughter of Mary McLeod Bethune, has chronicled the roots of her internal drive for personal excellence and her unselfish willingness to serve in the liberation struggle of our people. It has now become evident to me why Evelyn Bethune can't and won't stop seeking ways to solve the puzzle of black people's difficult circumstances. The hunger for knowledge and thirst for liberation is a part of her DNA.

The Holy Qur'an states *"speak not of those who die in the way of Allah (God) as being dead, nay they are alive but you perceive not."* This is to remind us that God's righteous servants never die; rather they will keep coming back in every generation until His universe is perfected. God never gets old; He is fresh in every generation the Honorable Minister Louis Farrakhan teaches us. As a student minister of the Honorable Minister Louis Farrakhan in the city of Houston, I have been privileged to meet Dr. Mary McLeod Bethune in the person of her granddaughter, Dr. Evelyn Bethune. I can personally bear witness to the truth that God's eternal spirit which moved through one Bethune at the turn of the twentieth century is still working in another Bethune at the turn of the twenty-first century.

As I reminisce about my own grandmother Dorothy Hall and her generation, I can't help but wonder what it was like to be black in America at the turn of the 20th century. What does this present generation need to do to reach the promise land of freedom, justice, and equality my grandmother's generation yearned for? *BETHUNE* provides a template for all to follow to achieve generational continuity of struggle and collective progress. This is a must read for anyone who is serious about human rights and dignity. We owe Dr. Evelyn Bethune an eternal debt of gratitude for this important contribution to understanding our great elder Dr. Mary McLeod Bethune's descendents. It is my prayer that through their stories our own path to liberation will become clearer.


Minister Robert Muhammad
Muhammad Mosque #45
4443 Old Spanish Trail
Houston, TX 77021

### *"Finally, I leave you a responsibility to our young people."*

I have always loved Mary McLeod Bethune from the first mention of her name in my 8th grade social studies class.  She was one of the precious few heroines' of African descent that the segregated school curriculums of the 1960's taught...  Founding a college with one dollar and fifty cents, selling sweet potato pies on the weekend...  Befriending a First Lady and advising her husband, the President of the United States...  Special Assistant to the Secretary of War during WWII...  They didn't tell us too much, but it was enough for me to fall in love with a woman who died the year I was born...

Much later, when I discovered her "Last Will and Testament", first published in Ebony Magazine in 1955, I was struck with the last one, in particular.  It aptly sums up my passion in the work I believe God ordained for my gifts and talents.  So when TIME Magazine named me a "Rising Star" for creating programs that teach the vast, varied and rich heritage of people of African descent, I specifically requested that Mary McLeod Bethune be publicly noted as a cherished historical mentor, whose work, vision and faith inspired, guided and motivated me from my inside place.

Needless to say, when the opportunity to meet her granddaughter was offered, my heart skipped a beat. For me, this was a lifetime moment.  After the introductions, Dr. Evelyn Bethune looked deeply in my eyes and said, "My grandmother is all over you..." I thought I would cry - and did so later. Sharing our stories over Sunday breakfast, the deal was sealed and friendship for a lifetime was made.

Since that time, Evelyn and I have lived our lives as dear friends, sharing the intimacies of two lives that are surely blessed beyond measure, in spite of- or probably because of -the highs and lows of two lives lived fully. Together, we have taught community classes and participated in conferences, shared great laughter and heart tears, moved from one state to another, planned, plotted and prayed all the way. Our shared earth journey is still in full force; together we continue working the work, knowing that there is not only great work to be done, but great joy to be shared. This is a joyful lifetime moment. So, it is with historical honor and contemporary gratitude that I share these reflections, knowing that the inspiring legacy of my historical mentor, Mary McLeod Bethune, is indeed being carried forward in this work called *BETHUNE.*

By Professor Melodye Micëre Van Putten, M.A.
Africalogist/Education Consultant
President & CEO, Black History Works, Inc.

# Prologue

*Greetings…*

Like most relatives of famous people, the grandchildren of Dr. Mary McLeod Bethune are often asked what it is like to be related to someone so well known. For me, the answer has never been an easy one. We called her Mother Dear and even today when we are speaking to each other about the things we remember, we always say "Mother Dear".

My grandmother was far ahead of her time in her vision, focus, and ability to lead our people. She placed the well being of the people far ahead of any ideas of self. Growing up in her shadow was sometimes the hardest aspect of my life and other times the most rewarding. I have learned patience as well as how to forgive. My faith has gone from a surface requirement to a deep connection with God that allows me to truly be at peace even in the midst of great difficulty. Throughout this life experience however, we were blessed with parents who taught us by example to give to others, to share no matter how little we might have, to love deeply and to trust God.

I can remember the sound of my grandmother's voice as she told stories to the neighborhood children at story hour on Saturday mornings. I can also remember the gentleness of her touch as she would sit me on her lap to simply be my grandmother. The smells of her house and love for family are a part of the comfort that comes in the memories.

My name is Evelyn Idell Bethune and the first female grandchild. I was born in Daytona Beach, FL, in the year 1952, by the grace of God and the prayers of my maternal great grandmother, Sara Jones. She prayed me into this world when the white "doctor" who was supposed to assist my mother with a difficult delivery, walked out on us as she lay in the delivery room trying to push me through pelvic hip bones that would not dilate. She should have had a cesarean-section (c-section) but remember that she was a black woman, in 1952, giving birth in a hospital that had little or no space for black people. The doctor said that he was tired and left my mother in the care of a black midwife who would not give up on us. With her help and the prayers of my momma Sara, my mother agonizingly pushed me into this world and lived to talk about it. Many people have told me this story as I was growing up and they always say that every sick person in the "colored Ward" got healed that day because momma Sara got on her knees and lifted up a prayer so powerful that God had to hear it and because she was a true prayer warrior, my momma and I lived. The story also goes a bit further to say that I came into the world unmarked by the trauma of my birth, not screaming but with a smile and eyes wide open. The elders would say "She was looking ahead of herself, seeing the unseen"; which was another way of saying that I came into the world already knowing, I would just have to remember.

When I think about that statement today, I know that I have insights and I don't remember a time that I did not feel the presence of God in my life even when I placed myself far from Him. This story is also a reminder to me that I have always been a fighter, unwilling to give up, even when the odds appear to not be in my favor. I call this '*In the spirit of Mary McLeod Bethune.*' God's almighty hand continued to guide me back to the right path and helped me not be afraid.

Years after my grandmother passed away, I also have other memories of sitting in the darkness of our house, because the lights had been turned off, looking out of the window of my parents bedroom at the lights of the college, the president's house, the dining hall, and science building, and wondering why everyone seemed to benefit from the work of my grandmother and my daddy, except for our family. When our lights would get turned off because my parents could only stretch their resources so far, we didn't understand how there could be so much and yet so little. When my father was forced to retire on a $50 a month pension we did not understand. Where was the care and compassion from the college to which he had given his life in order to help his mother realize her dream of providing an education for the descendants of the enslaved Africans? As he recovered from a stroke that nearly took his life, attempts were underway to distance him from the college that carried his last name, Bethune-Cookman College. This was the place where as a child, he had sold magnolia blossoms to tourists to help fund its growth, made ink from elderberries, raised chickens for food and grew vegetables. Yet the very institution that should have nurtured the descendants of its founder, pushed them away like unwelcome step children.

How do you come to a place of peace in your very soul when you see the legacy left to you being stolen away? The journey to the answer is a true tale of God at Work. It is the story of Mary's Grandbabies...out of the darkness of slavery into the light of freedom. You see, one does not always have to have a visible shackle to be enslaved. Sometimes the enslavement comes through fear and anger. This is the true story of coming out of that darkness into the light of freedom. It is a story of love and family and how the strength of our ancestors is with us and guides us to the restoration of stolen legacies.

For about 10 years I have thought about, talked about and started writing a book about life as one of the grand children of Mary McLeod Bethune. I thought about bringing in the historical content, interviewing my siblings and others community people who knew us when we were growing up, all the things you do when you are trying to gather information and get all the facts together for the greatest non-fictional work of the decade. Yet I could not get all the pieces to come together. Try as I might it seemed that there was always something in the way. Yet the driving desire to tell our story never went away. Now here I am feeling the urge to get this thing going because I know that there is a story to tell and in the telling there is also a healing.

I must remind you that this is my story, my point of view and my memory of events. It is told from the stand point of living the day to day with my parents, my brothers and sisters, my nieces and nephews and feeling what they felt. I have seen the impact of my grandmother on our lives. Her imprint is deep and wide. This book is also a lot of my feelings, good, bad, ugly, spiritual, and sometimes indifferent, but never empty of emotion. I talk a bit about Daytona and what it was like to grow up in a place seen by the outside world as what one of my professors called "a new South City". The Daytona in which I grew up was far from *new south* and took pride in being a solid, old south city. The "colored people" lived on one side of the rail road tracks and the white people on the other. As big as the ocean is, we could not swim on the "Worlds Most Famous Beach" until the late 60's and even then most of the Black people that I knew still did not go to the beach in Daytona to socialize. There are some who will declare that not much has changed.

This is the story, our story, of how to never give up, even in the face of what seems like insurmountable obstacles. Never give up, never, never, never, never, never, never, never, never, never, never, never, ever.

***In the Spirit of Dr. Mary McLeod Bethune***
***Doc***

# BETHUNE

## Out of Darkness into the Light of Freedom

# No Weapon

# Formed Against

# Me

# Shall Prosper

*"If we accept and acquiesce in the face of discrimination, we accept the responsibility ourselves. We should, therefore, protest openly everything ... that smacks of discrimination or slander."*
**Mary McLeod Bethune**

The mysterious box stared ominously back at me as I carefully set it down on the table. I felt an instant icy chill down my spine when my eyes focused on the return address: Gainesville, FL. It was from the University. My heart began to beat a little faster. What could I possibly be receiving from there that would require it be wrapped so carefully? So much time had been invested in burying painful memories and feelings from the past. I was finally able, in the recent years to breathe again, and now it was all being undone. All it took was one simple little box to open the floodgate.

I was still not aware of what lie within the package as I pushed it away. I could not bring myself to open it, not yet. A myriad of memories were flowing over me like waves, both good and bad. I found my meditation chair and collapsed into it. "Deep breaths E," I whispered to myself over and over. "E" was a nickname given to me from long ago. I closed my eyes and focused on taking in and releasing air very slowly and rhythmically. Perhaps it was time to let go and allow everything to just take over me. "You cannot be free until you release all that is hidden deep within." Through the whirlwind of emotions, I heard those words echo in my mind. This was a bondage from which I desired freedom.

I continued my breathing exercises for a few minutes longer. I had learned some years back how to meditate during my prayer time, and also during moments of great stress. This definitely counted as one of those times. The meditation always helped me to calm my body and remain focused in my mind. When stress would try to slither in, it assisted me to regain clarity. Most importantly, God had been at my side throughout my life. Whether I was standing on top of a mountain or crawling through a valley, He had me in His hands. My thumping heart was gradually returning to its normal pace. I could feel the warmth of my heavenly Father encompass me. My eyes opened as the memories began to resend, like the ocean waters at low tide. The box was still sitting on the table unopened. I eased out of my chair and made my way to it with a mixed sense of caution and curiosity. What could they possibly have sent me? I carefully opened the box and pulled out a beautiful glass sculpture. It was an award of appreciation for all of my hard work and dedication to the Institute of Black Culture. I ran my hands over the etched words of thanks, wanting to laugh and cry at the same time. I was sent an award for the very work I spent a year being persecuted for. There was an instant desire to smash the sculpture into thousands of tiny pieces.

This beautiful token was certainly not big enough to close the wound that would not stop bleeding. My initial thought was *too little, too late*. Anger had been clawing to get inside my heart for months, and it almost succeeded. I never believed that my grandmother would have been disappointed regarding the trial because she would know that I was standing my ground. But now to allow myself to be consumed by hatred and unforgiveness would have greatly saddened her. I loved her, my family and myself too much to let that happen.

Memories and images were no longer soaring through my mind. I was remembering better times, when there were expectations and new horizons. I was remembering one of the happiest times in my life. That time was also connected to receiving a package from the University. I felt a smile spread across my lips. It was my acceptance letter from the University of Florida for graduate school. Sometimes it seems as if that day just occurred; before the drama, pain and lawsuits. At this moment in time, none of the drama has happened – I am still at the dawn of this new chapter in my life. Receiving that letter was possibly one of the most exciting events of my life. I remember my hands slightly shaking just staring at the envelope. I had every confidence that I would be accepted, but I was still so nervous. What if they said no? But how could they, it was divined by God.

The envelope was so crisp and official that I almost did not want to open it. I must have read over those words at least a dozen times. As soon as I saw "congratulations" my heart soared. At that very moment nothing else mattered; I was finally in. I knew the ancestors would be proud, especially Mother Dear. It was as if her mantle was being passed to me. Although I knew I had the anointing for what God placed in my heart to do, I needed to be credentialed as well. I would have the opportunity to earn my doctoral degree in political science. My goal was to hopefully open the eyes of young people and bring political and economic awareness to newer generations who were fast forgetting upon whose backs they were standing.

The decision to enter graduate school, and the acceptance letter that followed were milestones for me in so many ways. They symbolized a mountain top, after spending so much time wandering in the wilderness and trudging through valleys. Sometimes it feels as though there are two of me; one that has experienced all of the pleasure and the other that has suffered the pain. The year I began my doctoral studies was 1992. The months and years leading to my initial decision to attend grad school were sometimes filled with great pain as well as incredible joy. For example, 1989 was a year filled with so much grief and loss. First the deaths, my husband Julius, then my oldest sister Theodora, followed that same year by my daddy and then in 1990 by my mother.

Up to this point, I had not experienced the death of anyone this close to me since the death of Charles West Miller when I was in high school. Charles was full of life and so talented. No one could imitate James Brown better than Charles and he died in Vietnam way ahead of his time. I loved him so very much. I can still remember my daddy taking me to school and we would see Charles hitching a ride to the airport because his car had broken down. This was February 1968. Charles had gotten drafted right out of high school and he was shipping out to Vietnam. My dad pulled over and gave Charles a ride to the airport. How could we know that the next time we saw him would be at his funeral in April? Two months later, Charles was killed as he fought in a war that never should have been. He was 19 years old and full of life until the end. That's what I remembered about death until liver cancer took my husband of 8 years, so quickly that we had little time to say good bye. That was May of 1989.

In August of the same year my beloved sister, Theodora dies of a brain aneurism. She gave every ounce of her being to the care and happiness of others, taking very little time to give to herself. That is what killed her. Instead of taking time to go to the doctor to keep her blood pressure under control, she cared for grandchildren, nieces and neighborhood children. She took care of grown children who should have been caring for her and none of us thought to check and make sure that she was alright because she never complained. She had a spirit of light and she loved to laugh. My sister was a joy in my life that I will never be able to replace and I thank God everyday that he thought enough of me to allow me to laugh and sing with her and best of all to watch her dance.

In October of 1989, after almost 91 years of life, my daddy joined the ancestors who watch over me. My mother used to say, of all the things my daddy loved, he loved me best; even more that he loved her. When I was born, my daddy only had one other child at that time, my brother Albert, Jr. who is 32 years older than me. My mother said that when he knew he had a baby girl, he was so filled with joy. When I was old enough, he'd put me in the car seat, and I went every where with him. The beauty of having a parent who is retired is that they have more time to spend with you. That was our daddy. I remember taking my first baby steps on the training field for Bethune-Cookman's football team. During football season, father would drive over to the training field, which was just down the street from our house, to watch the team practice and talk with his friends. The men of the community, the young boys, and the college students, got an opportunity to come together. This was second only to the barbershop or beauty salon as a place to share information and fellowship. The band would also practice around this time so the air was filled with music and the energy of a football game. It had to be the best way to grow up. I learned to love football and community.

As I grew older, I felt a closer bond to my father than my mother, and I can remember many times, as a teenager, thinking that my mother might love me, but she really didn't like me. This was a feeling that carried into my adult years but I feel very fortunate that my mother and I were able to really talk through my pain and hers before she died. Although she died after the others, she was sick with cancer long before it took her life.

Imagine you are standing almost waist deep in the ocean. Suddenly and unexpectedly, a wave rises up out of the calm water and hurdles over you without any hint of mercy. Sputtering and wet, you stumble to your feet just in time for another wave to drive you back down. It was one wave right after the other. By this point you are out of breath; physically spent and have likely swallowed far more sea water than you really care to. Your confidence has also been shaken, causing you to doubt whether you would be able to stand back up or not. That was me; cold, wet and weary of all the cares and trials that continued to crash into me. My family was enduring many of the same storms. On the outside, we had our armor in place and appeared to be moving forward in timely fashion. But deep inside these strong coats of armor, we were but fragile children. In public we stood strong, but in the privacy of our homes, we limped along.

I felt a familiar tightness in my chest, but forced myself to remain calm. Throughout the months of grief, I was the person everyone looked to for support and guidance. I was the "Rock" for the family, and rocks are never supposed to crumble. It was very exhausting to have to mask my own sadness in order to comfort others, but it also postponed my having to confront my loss and accept the reality of my loved ones' departure. My duty to my family had also become my crutch. The year following the deaths was a haze for me. I worked, slept and ate; in other words, I merely functioned. The zeal that life held for me seemed to have vanquished. I was trying to pretend that this hadn't really happened; it was only a bad dream and eventually, I would wake up. In the process and bustle of assuring that the other members of my family were okay, I neglected to tend to my own broken heart until the day it finally gave out.

It does not seem so long ago that I was still living in

Miami and enjoying a very busy lifestyle of running my own healthcare management business called HOME, Inc. From its inception, my company had been rather blessed with favor, opened doors and an abundance of good clients. There were certainly some trials and tribulations, but I always knew that my heavenly Father was watching over me. I believe that even my location was the result of divine intervention. HOME, Inc. was in one of the newer areas of Miami and housed in the newest high rise on Brickell Ave at the time. These were the type of prime spots reserved for shiny white business men with more cash than morals and I was an African American woman. When we made the cover of Florida Trends Magazine we gave thanks and felt like nothing could go wrong. The company was doing so well that by the late eighties, we were in the beginning stages of forming a unique kind of HMO comprised entirely of African American physicians.

Even though I was separated from my husband, (Julius #2), I was moving along so smoothly; my two beautiful daughters were quickly turning into amazing young women; life finally looked promising. Julius was still in California but we were talking about reconciliation and loving each other over the phone. Then the bottom fell out. He took sick and with me in Miami, I had no idea how sick. In a matter of months he was hospitalized and I got a phone call that said he might not make it. I could not believe my ears. How could that be possible? One week I was talking to him daily and he was great and planning to visit and next the doctors don't think he will live long enough for me to get to Sacramento. As my plane touched down in

Sacramento, I knew that Julius was slipping away. I could not catch my breath and felt like my heart was bursting and then there was peace. I went to the hospital and they allowed me to see him before his body was removed to the funeral home. It was probably one of the most difficult moments that I have ever experienced. I went back to my hotel and spent the next day remembering our brief time together. He was a wonderful man and I gave thanks for the blessing of having spent time with him. In our relationship, he was not the problem, I was. I was determined to run everything. All the women in my life have been exceedingly strong and very strong willed. I did not know how to let a man be a man. It took me another 10 years to figure it out. His death was the first to blindside me. Everything came to a crashing halt that day. How was I to know that within a few months I would have walked away from all that I worked so hard for in a futile effort to save those whose time on this earth was already coming to a close?

Imagine that you are in the middle of a war zone and both sides are riddling the air with bullets. There is a searing pain that rips through your side and you realize that you have just been shot. But in the midst of the pain and fear, you remember your children. Suddenly your wounds are secondary to making sure your babies are okay. You would crawl through broken glass if necessary to protect them. I was more concerned with the well-being of my daughters' than myself. Life itself was suddenly much more fragile than before. My parents were ill for some time and I was now very aware of just how easily they could slip away from me. After my husband's funeral, I walked away from the life I had built in Miami and returned home to care for my father and mother. The year before my mother was diagnosed with lung cancer though she never smoked a day in her life. I will always believe that her cancer came from breathing the carcinogens that were in the smoke of pressing and curling hair with products made from petroleum. The "hair grease" used to keep those curls in place and make that "nappy" hair hold a style, had serious side effects and we will probably never know how many of our illnesses came from their use.

I returned home just in time to mourn the loss of my oldest sister, Theodora. Part of me was still reeling from the last funeral, and I was now helping to plan a second one. Theodora died of a brain aneurism and the loss of her beauty and her loving ways is still felt deeply. My sister loved to dance and I know that she is enjoying herself with all the great musicians who may have found their way into heaven. Her death coming right behind that of Julius really rocked my family. I believe this is when my heart began to close itself off from the rest of the world. Then before I could exhale, daddy died and my spirit struggled to find sustenance.

My unwillingness to take care of myself emotionally caused me to lose much time with my children and remaining family. It also led to a very hasty decision to remarry. I do not believe that everyone realized how much additional pressure they placed on me. I was looking for relief, and I wanted to be loved again. Thomas ("Tom") both loved and needed me in a way that my family did not. It was like an escape from the harshness that entered my life several months before. I truly believed that I loved him and that he could make me happy. I was very wrong. Had I simply waited a few months longer, I would have seen firsthand his addiction to crack cocaine. Instead of turning tail as many probably would have advised, I stood by my new spouse and helped him throughout his stay in rehab.

We were barely newlyweds and already there was chaos and drama. Nevertheless, I showed my support by attending meetings with Thomas and researching a mountain of information regarding addictions. My already fragile emotions were now speeding down the tumultuous tracks of one menacing roller coaster after another. I went from being angry at him for putting me through all of this, to missing him, and also wondering if I was somehow the catalyst that caused this problem with my husband. All I could do was pray and hope that this would be his final stay in rehab.

There is a saying that God will always meet you halfway. I disagree. God will meet you where you are. If you only take one step, I know He will make up the other ninety-nine. And it has more to do with your heart than any steps at all. You have to desire His help more than anything else. No one can change the character of a man but God. After two more trips to rehab with Thomas, doors being kicked in by a man, crazed with a crack cocaine addiction and the fear of abuse, I had to realize there was not anything in my own strength that I could do to help

Thomas. His love for me was not greater than his love for cocaine, and sadly, I did not love him enough to waste what was left of my heart on someone who did not want to change. On his fourth trip back to the rehabilitation center, I informed Thomas of my intention to end our marriage. I packed up all of his belongings and told him I would always care and pray for him. I just could not stay married to him. Every fiber in me wanted to weep and scream at the same time. I had maxed myself out, both emotionally and financially trying to be all things to all people. I truly did not know what to do next, or even where I could go. I felt so very alone for the first time in nearly two years. The grief had finally clawed its way out of my heart and into my entire body. Now I could not feel anything but that cold mournful cage. All I could think was how badly I needed to rest.

I left Thomas that day and headed directly to North Carolina where my brother Hobson was stationed in the Marine Corps. I wanted to be somewhere that would allow me to clear my head and decide my next course of action. For my own sake, I had to be selfish and think of myself first. There was so much of me that was broken and I needed time to heal. My wonderful brother did not once prod me for the reason of my visit. He simply opened his arms and home to me the minute I arrived.

I spent a little over a month with Hobson and his family, doing nothing else except sleeping and eating. Between naps and meals, I was on my knees in prayer. I was also weighing my options for employment and whether or not to stay in North Carolina or go back home to Daytona Beach. Most of my life had been dedicated to living up to the expectations of others. While I would not change anything I had achieved, much of my work and accomplishments were not for me. When the people for whom I strived so hard for passed away, I was left feeling empty and without direction. I watched my father always put aside his own dreams and desires for someone else. It was finally time to stop following in his footsteps and do something for myself.

As I began to seek God on what I should do, He was already slowly pulling away the layers of hurt and stress from my mind and heart that had been concealing His path for my life. God showed me two dreams that I had desired to fulfill for years, but never completed, and that is to teach and get my doctorate degree. I felt as if the clouds parted and the sunshine filled the sky. The Bible says that God orders the steps of His children, and I knew He was doing just that for me. Hope was flowing through me again. I was so excited about my decision to enter graduate school that I wanted to herald my news from the mountain tops. For almost a decade I had been putting off returning to school. With all of the change that had been clamoring through my life over the past few years, I knew this was the season for taking new steps. Although I would always miss Tee, and Julius, Mommy and Daddy, I knew it was also time to put aside the sack cloth and ashes. After all, the Bible says that we are not to mourn but rather rejoice for we know we will see them again soon. I could just imagine my daddy seeing Mother Dear as he entered heaven. What a family reunion. That image brought a smile to my face and comfort to my heart.

I cleared the initial hurdle of what I wanted to do with the rest of my life, but now I needed to decide where to go and how to pay for it. Despite the fact that my savings account was almost bone dry and I was working, I was completely assured that God would make a way where there seems to be no way. As I was weighing my options, I received word from my youngest daughter that she would soon be giving birth to my first grandchild. I decided to return to Florida to help her into motherhood. My focus on graduate schools was already shifting to my home state. Bethune-Cookman did not offer graduate degrees at the time so I made a list of possibilities. The next step was to look at financing and entrance requirements. I had always been a good student so I wasn't worried too much about grades, and although taking the GRE was not one of my favorite things to do, I knew I could pass it if I studied. My list of schools was quickly shortened to Howard University and the University of Florida. I always believed and trusted God to open the doors that no man can close and also for financial blessing to pay for my schooling. It is funny how small we think sometimes. I was requesting just enough to squeak by from the God who says He will supply all of our needs according to His riches in glory. He chose to bless me with His best instead of what I thought I deserved. As I prepared to re-enter the world, I took the GRE, figuring that I would take it, get my grades back and then study the areas that needed improvement. I would take it again and then submit the best grade to admissions. But the God I serve helped me get it right the first time. I was so anxious about taking the test I threw up on my way to the testing center. I prayed to calm my system enough for me to take the test and managed to get through it. I knew I had done well but I did not know that I made the score I needed until a month later. When I recount moments like these, I call them 'God at Work Moments" because they absolutely have nothing to do with my ability. These moments are opportunities for God to show us that He is with us and working on our behalf. To God be the glory!

I was over the moon simply to be accepted by the University of Florida and Howard, but there was so much more to come. It was the University of Florida however that offered a full ride with a Presidential fellowship that included a monthly stipend. God met my needs and then some! This was also further confirmation that I was moving in the right direction. There was much to do in preparation to begin my graduate studies. I needed to leave North Carolina and get ready to begin school during the summer of 1992. That was just about a year away, but time passes quickly when you are preparing for a life changing experience. This was getting to be exciting. This meant that I really needed to get my mental self in order and get ready to be a full time student for the next few years. That also meant preparing to be broke.

As I left Camp LaJeune, NC., I had other reasons to be excited as I was about to become a grandmother for the first time. There have been many times that I have tried to describe my feelings about being a grandmother. Words are inadequate when I think of how to describe the love I have for my grandson. I love my daughters more than the breath I need to live but they both know that CJ *is* the very breath I need to live. As Marcia prepared to bring new life into the world I was preparing to begin life again too. Upon returning to Daytona, I moved in with Marcia and Charles in the hope of spending as much time as possible caring for my daughter and my soon to be grandchild. At the time, I did not know if it was a girl or boy and I really did not care. I was just praying for a healthy child. My daughter joyously welcomed a healthy baby into the world in August 1991. It was so amazing to hold my grandson and envision his promise and potential. At the same time of adding life to my family, I had to finish removing the death. An annulment for my marriage was filed and granted in 1992 prior to beginning classes that summer.

There was so much time in my life to be redeemed. I was not about to waste anymore on just coasting through school. I put my nose to the grind and pushed forward. It was very different to be back in classes after all this time. Many of the other students were ten and fifteen years my junior. Even a few professors were younger than me. And while I was thankful for the opportunity extended to me by the University, I could not help but notice the obvious racial inequalities that existed. The city of Gainesville was not known for its color blind residents; in fact it was quite the opposite, I could clearly see the double standard that was presented from the student government and the faculty towards white students versus black students. Perhaps this was my reason for being in this school and at this time, to push for change, for diversity and equal treatment. I came from a line of strong women and it was not in me to be silent in the face of wrong doing. I became very vocal about my views and opinions on civil rights.

I remember the first time I met University President Lombardi. He commented how my name was in the paper more often than his and he was the school's president. As I stated earlier, I was not shy about making myself heard. There was a lack of support for African American students in the Political Science department as well. I questioned the department head why there were not any black teachers. He replied that good candidates never presented themselves. I pressed this issue until possibly frustrated; he began searching specifically for African American political science professors. Imagine his surprise at the bumper crop of excellent candidates. I could not wait to finish my studies and begin my own teaching career.

I was completing the requirements for my master's and doctorate degrees when a unique and seemingly perfect job offer was presented to me. In 1993 the Director of Student Affairs asked me to be the Assistant Director of the University's Institute of Black Culture. This was a tailor-made job for me; I would have the chance to bring appreciation and pride of African heritage to many black students who may have never known where they came from. I asked for a few adjustments in the hiring proposal. One of those adjustments was the support of the department in cleaning up and revitalizing the Institute. He agreed and almost without hesitation, I accepted the extended offer.

On the outside, the Institute of Black Culture was a beautifully sculpted building with giant pillars and a manicured lawn. On the inside however, it was a shag carpet nightmare. Ugly orange carpet covered the place literally head to toe, or floor to ceiling in this case. The air was musty and reeked of mildew. It was old, dark and cramped. The man who presided as director for the past twenty years was also a full time pastor in a local church and I am sure he was tired of fighting the battle for resources and at some point gave up. I was filled with ideas and frustration at the same time. This unkempt building with virtually no budget was a perfect example of how the University neglected its non-white population. My first official day was spent observing and making notes of what the Institute would need in order to revive itself. I spoke with the library about ordering books and other reading materials to place in the Institute. I presented the student government with a proposal to assist in the renovation, which was quickly approved as it had the support of the treasurer and the SGA president.

The work began. Facilities management gave as much as they could and the craftsmen of the city as well as University workmen felt the spirit of this project and put their all into making it work. The old carpet was pulled out to reveal both water damage and several hidden windows. Between my job and classes, I stayed busy much of the day. The approved budget for the Institute probably tripled from what it was before. The restoration project grew somewhat from the original plans. We decided to tear down one wall and widen the staircase. Of course this meant the installation of a beautiful banister and the refinishing of the wooden stairs. We moved bookcases, to find and repair water damaged walls. I found a local shop that specialized in selling African inspired décor to make window treatments. Windows were added to the upstairs porch and it was enclosed to add meeting space to a small dark room that took on a life filled with light. A few artists from around the area agreed to showcase some of their work. This was a magnificent project that would last as well as heal.

I view what I did for the Institute of Black Culture as a work of love. I wanted to make it a place where young African Americans would spend time and learn about themselves. As the assistant director, I was able to make purchases and submit the receipts for reimbursement. Not at any time was I able to approve any of these purchases nor did I write the checks. I did not have final approval for anything at the Institute. Weeks of work and renovations were finally coming to a close. We held a grand re-opening for the newly redesigned Institute of Black Culture with very successful results. Everyone praised the new look, and the library located in the back. Just as I hoped, students began to socialize in and around the building. Professors used the Institute for class sessions and a few exhibits were held there as well. I could not have been more proud, if it were my own house.

I was completely unaware of what was to come. In 1994, the University formally accused and charged me with misappropriating funds from the Institute of Black Culture. I was in Atlanta when I learned that a warrant had been issued for my arrest. I was in shock and very confused. How did they think I managed to pull this off? I did not have the authority to approve any payments, and reimbursements had to go through two or three levels of approval before checks were cut. I also was not the person cutting the checks. Every item purchased for the Institute was located in The Institute of Black Culture and as far as I know is still there. I could not believe this was happening. My voice was numb and distant as I asked what should be done. I decided to return to Florida to formally surrender. My brother Hobson promised he would have a bond to immediately get me back out. I arrived at the designated precinct house and took care of paperwork and other business related to the warrant. My bond was ready, as promised and I was told I could leave. All I wanted to do was crawl in bed and sob.

I was barely out of the door when officers ushered me back inside and rearrested me. This time it was for violation of my probation in Volusia County. When it rains it pours as the saying goes. I was remanded to custody and had to wait for transport to Volusia County. This took a day or so and just happened to be on a holiday weekend, so I was to spend the holiday (Easter I believe) in the Volusia county jail. Although I could have been released on an ROI, the prosecutor would not agree to any other judge hearing the case and because the original judge was on holiday, I was kept in jail. My brother was livid, but there was not anything he could do.

Turned out that the original judge, Judge Gayle S. Graziano, was having her own problems with the State of Florida, and my case was turned over to another judge in Volusia County anyway. This of course came after I spent two weeks in jail. A court date was set for the probation violation hearing in mid December 1995. The new judge stated that he felt an example needed to be made and that the previous judge had been too lenient. I was sentenced to sixty days in jail and given 30 days to report. This was mid December, fear could have easily filled my heart if I wasn't careful. I remembered how Joseph must have felt after his master Potiphar had him thrown in prison over trumped up charges – just like me. What did Joseph do? He prayed and continued to serve God. I decided to do just that and it was not long before things began to change for me.

Women started coming to me for help and advice. I was fortunate to be able to afford a lawyer for my case, but many of those girls had the court appointed legal aid that was more about closing cases as fast as they could than really offering any aid. I also got to teach like I had desired to; it was not how I envisioned, but it was so much more fulfilling than I realized. The other inmates were hungry for any morsel of knowledge they could get into their heads. It was a very surreal experience for me and for my family. When I was locked up in the county jail, I wrote in my journals daily and continued to trust God. Melody Micere Stewart VanPuttan was my life line. She allowed me to call her daily, she and Pastor Sheldon Shipman of Walls Memorial A.M.E. Zion Church in Charlotte, SC would pray with me on the phone. I wrote on the outside of one of my journals, "They can lock me up but they can't lock God Out". That is true whether you are in physical jail or mental jail. God is always there, we have but to call on the name of Jesus. I prayed and studied the Word with a renewed intensity and found strength in God. After forty five days, I was released for good behavior. Imagine that!

My stay in jail was over, but the fight for my freedom was just beginning. Every emotion was surging throughout my body as I returned home. I knew that I was being wrongfully accused and was determined to fight tooth and nail to clear my name. The media was already circling the story like a school of blood thirsty sharks. It was not enough just to plaster my name all over their slanderous articles; the headlines that read "granddaughter of Mary McLeod Bethune" hit me like hundreds of tiny needles in my heart. I was not ever ashamed for myself, but for the negative impact this lawsuit was having on Mother Dear's name and legacy. This angered me as much as those incredulous charges. I wanted to proclaim my innocence to as many people as I could. I kept waiting for those who knew that I never stole anything or received any personal gain from the expenditures, to step forward. I kept thinking that this could not possibly be happening. I was mistaken and I waited in vane. I was also too silent on my own behalf and did not fight my fight. I allowed the advice of others to place me in unfamiliar territory.

I paid a high price for not listening to my inner self. I had always been in the forefront when dealing with issues no matter how tough, and here I was in a fight for my life and I was silent. I was afraid and I was intimidated because I was on unfamiliar ground. I also could not wrap my mind around how one month I am being awarded as an outstanding student, inducted into the University Student Hall of Fame, Florida Blue Key Honor Society and really feeling like my life is coming together again and suddenly everything changes and things are falling apart.

I was advised by my legal counsel to keep my personal feelings in check and allowed this to be played out in the courtroom. I was told to not give interviews or allow it to be tried in the press. It was too late for that. The press had a mind all its own and my silence only seemed to fuel the fire. I believed that I would be vindicated in the course of the trial and that my attorney would really fight for me and prove to all that I was not a thief. I will never forget his words to me just before the hearing began, "So what do you think we should do?" My heart sunk a little because I found out too late that he was not a litigator at least not for me. He was just doing his job. Part of me wanted to reach over and literally shake the sense back into him. Another part of me wanted to run away and scream. But I did neither; I turned and walked into the building as if I had not heard a single word he said.

How long can you fight when you are the only one on your side with a sword in your hand? This legal skirmish became a battle that waged for a little over a year. The dollar amount that the University of Florida accused me of "misappropriating" dropped from $100,000 to

$6,000 before the trial was even underway; this was beyond insanity. I kept thinking that somewhere in the midst of the insanity the truth would be clear and all this would go away; this was not about to happen. The newspapers were without mercy in their coverage of the lawsuit and upcoming trial. My soul felt battered and cut, but I was determined not to let go, until my name was cleared.

I could take anything that was thrown at me. If I were the only one being affected, I could fight until I either won or keeled over. But my daughters were being harassed and receiving phone calls regarding the trial. It was too painful to see my children and the rest of my family getting the backlash for my drama and it had to stop. It was never a question of whether they were willing to endure the attention; my girls wanted to be on the front lines with me. But It was my decision, and as a mother I needed to not put them through any more pain. I also did not have the right legal counsel. My attorney, though good at what he did, I did not feel that he fought for me in the way that I knew he could. In the end, he really may have felt that a plea bargain was the best way out as I was out of money. There are many people who would never understand why I accepted the plea offer. To them, and to the rest of the world, it meant that I must be guilty. Those people have never had to be a mother and be in my position. *"Let he who is without sin..."*

As I read the beautiful glass, etched with words of appreciation, I had a sudden rush of emotions that ran from rage to a feeling of peaceful closure. It was as if this beautiful glass token was trying to close a gaping wound that didn't want to stop bleeding. Here I was, awaiting closure to a criminal lawsuit against me, filed by the University and they were sending me an acknowledgment of their appreciation for the love and care that I placed in the Institute. Part of me was saying: Too Little, Too late" But the other part of me was saying "Thank you". Thank you to those who remembered how much I loved and cared for the Institute, my colleagues, my students, and yes, even the University. This was exciting stuff or at least the media thought so. But the path is never straight nor the load easy. Yet like the grandmother before me, the true test of my faith was yet to come.

I remember the feeling I had when I gave up and accepted the offer. It was like I had been separated from my very soul. It was a pain I would carry to this day. I would not serve any jail time, but five years probation and a felony on my record. The judge tried to chide me for my supposed actions, stating that he was sure that my grandmother would be ashamed of me for using the influence of her name to cause harm. However, I refused to take his lashing silently and narrowly escaped being held in contempt of court. Some would say that it was finally over, but the truth was, it would never really be over as the "Scarlett Letter" would always be there for those who would seek my destruction. Again I knew I would have to trust in God to get me through this dark place. It was during this time that I really discovered how much my sister and brothers, and my children really loved me. It was as if they wrapped me in a warm blanket of that love and stood for me when I could not stand for myself, but the affect of this decision to not fight a system that I truly felt was unjust would last a very long time.

When you become a convicted felon, some friends and many acquaintances see you differently and treat you in a manner that says "guilty". Even people that knew me well and saw how hard I worked approached me with a spirit of doubt. It was not long before I realized that I would have to create my own business and source of income because once you go on probation with a felony conviction, your whole life changes and opportunities disappear. I am eternally grateful that the spirit of my grandmother resides in me and that I was able to push through the dark places. I did it because I knew that even in the dark, God can find you. I promised myself that from this point forward, I would never allow a wrong to go unnoticed or hold my peace, when I knew an action was unjust. I decided that if I would be punished either way, it would not be because I just accepted injustice and gave up. Never again would that be an option.

I laid the glass award back inside the box. I was going to keep it. Someone thought enough of my work to recommend me for acknowledgment, and then to send me a sign that I could see – someone remembered how much I loved the Institute, and how much I loved the University and my students. Regardless of what the newspapers reported or how the administration felt, much of the student body stood behind me the entire time. To this day, when I encounter students who were at U of FL during that time, without exception, I am encouraged by the love and respect that they give. I helped bring about lasting changes that will have an impact for years to come to the culture of the University of Florida. And I found my strength in God. As my great grandmother Patsy McLeod would say, "It will not always be this way" and she surely has been proven right.

During this ordeal life continued, I moved to Atlanta and began working for a company called Silk 2. It is one of the largest Black owned and operated hair care products manufacturing and retail businesses in the country. Johns Searles, the CEO and founder is probably one of the most brilliant men in the world and through all of the news headlines and calls for interviews, he and his family and staff helped me to have some normalcy.

My life in Atlanta grew from working for someone else to administering community development as the project Director for the South DeKalb Small Business Incubator. It was one of the most rewarding and challenging projects I have directed. I was instrumental in assisting many small business owners in qualifying and receiving block grant money to upgrade their facade and signage, making them more attractive to the public thus improving their image and increasing their business.

I also joined the Pan African Orthodox Christian Church (PAOC)-Shrine of the Black Madonna located in the West End area of Atlanta and found the place where my political views and my Christian beliefs could be expressed in the same location. The African centered order of living and praising is a part of my spirit and was as natural to me as breathing. My African name is Serwa Kokumo Tuponelei, meaning, a noble woman, this one will not die, we are saved. The ceremony to change my name was one the most beautiful experiences of my life and will ever be a part of me. The PAOCC was founded by Albert Cleage, father of Pearl Cleage, in Detroit, Michigan because he felt that the church needed to be more active in the political arena and the decision making processes of life for the Africans in America. He was a genius at organizing young people and immersed them in the theology and thesis of our history based on the scriptures and the politics of the day.

The Shrine is a Christian based church built on the fundamentals of Black Theology and empowerment. It is also an organization that believes in communalism... giving as you have resources and receiving as you have need.

In February 1999 I fell down a flight of stairs at my home and spent 6 months recovering from a severely broken ankle, which required a plate to repair. Because I had no health insurance and no stop-gap insurance, I went back to work in a wheel chair and truly gained new appreciation for people living with disabilities. The simplest things became extremely difficult and soon the fact that I was on probation became an issue because it was a way out of my contract. I began to build a clientele of my own for small business development and started the Mary McLeod Bethune Family Legacy Foundation. I realized that it was critical to organize our family. I didn't realize it would take so long. Even though the business was doing ok, I still felt a deep need to be connected closer to God, and I also was at a place in my life that I knew I needed to get in touch with myself for myself. I had spent most of my life living for everyone else and trying to please the world only to discover that no matter what you do, someone will not be happy. You have to please God first. Everything after that is butter.

I moved out of my house onto the property owned by the Shrine, and in the year 2000 I became a full time Missionary. I was searching for the answer to my questions about my faith as well as a place to belong. My children were grown and doing fine and I was really feeling that "empty nest" syndrome. I have always been a giver and wanted a way to put more back into a community that seemed to have an endless need. I began my total immersion in the Shrine with a desire to learn how to drive a tractor.

I was transferred from Atlanta to Calhoun Falls, SC where the Shrine owns a 5000 acre farm called Beulah Land. This is property that was once farmed by enslaved Africans and after the Civil war much of the land was owned by these same black people, only to have it taken from them through deceit and murder. To walk that land and know that it was back in the hands of the descendents of the African diaspora was a wonderful feeling. Many times in the quiet of the morning or the late evening you could feel the spirit of the ancestors or even hear the laughter of the children that used to be. In an area call the Ginn Mill, their presence was so strong that many times it was over powering to the emotions. It was like you could feel the pain of slavery yet the satisfaction of them knowing the land were still theirs. All of the properties owned by the Shrine are debt free and sustained by good people who believe that the way to freedom is to own the institutions and be able to provide the basic needs of life for yourself and others.

For a little more than a year, I lived and worked on the land. Living in close quarters with other Missionaries taught us how to step outside of our own needs and be sensitive to the needs of others. We had communal meals and shared virtually every moment of the day with fellow Missionaries. I learned how strong I was and that I could adapt to any given situation. I learned to heard goats, inoculate cattle and assisted in the birthing of foals. I also learned how to clean a horse barn and feed cattle. I have dug fence posts and strung barbed wire, cut down trees and planted replacements. I also helped build houses on land so beautiful that you could not every doubt the power and glory of God. There was something very special about worshipping on Sunday morning in a building that has your initials in the foundation. I got married on Beulah Land to Fletcher King (Donkor) and for a wonderful moment we worked side by side to build a better kingdom for God. But all is not Jubilee, even in Gods land. Donkor was unfaithful and in a community as close as ours, there was no way for it to be a secret so our marriage failed and I had to worship sitting next to my sister in Christ who was sleeping with my husband. Finally Donkor left the farm and moved back to his home town of Houston only to find out that he was very ill and had to be hospitalized. He was in the V.A. Hospital for a couple of weeks when I got a phone call that he was really in need of someone to speak on his behalf as the doctors were really not doing anything and his white blood cell count was extremely low. It was so low that though he was able to get around and felt fine on most days, they did not want him to leave the hospital because of fear he might bump himself and hemorrhage to death by accident. I rode the Greyhound Bus from Calhoun Falls, S.C. to Houston, TX... This was a 28 hour ordeal and I know God gave me cool points for effort. I then proceeded to take care of my husband. He survived by having his spleen removed and we tried to resuscitate our marriage and finally gave up after struggling for another 18 months. Though our daily lives were immersed in service to the community and to God, there was little in place to help marriages survive and there were moments when I felt further from God within the Shrine than I did before I joined.

At the Shrine in Houston I was a teacher and assistant administrator for the Alkebu-lan Academy which is the home school for the Shrine. Bishop Aminata Ojore was the Principal and one of the most incredible women of honor that I have ever met. I learned so much under her leadership as it relates to early childhood development. Love is one of the most important ingredients in effective teaching. The education of children is one of the most critical challenges of the day across the country and especially in the Black community and the Shrine has it down to a science in theory. The reality was somewhat different as the children became older and had more interaction outside of the protective walls of the PAOCC.

After about 2 years the Academy was closed or placed on hiatus and I took on other duties and responsibilities within the administration of the PAOCC. But like most organizations, churches included, sometimes it is best to just be a member in the pews and not see the wizard behind the screen. I parted from the Shrine in 2004 with very few resources but an incredible faith in God. God had placed in my path all the resources that I would need when it was time for me to step out. I knew very little about Houston until the year before I moved off the property but as it became evident to me that I was going to become more independent, I started to venture out and learn my way around as well as meet new people. I discovered a community of Bethune-Cookman Alumni as well as many people from my home town of Daytona Beach. Among them are Sandra and Harold Strachan, Thomas Jones and the Law family, and many others who helped to make the transition easier. God opened a door so that I could find my way.

Today I am planning the rest of my life, and the family is excited about the possibilities as we organize to promote the love of family and the power of a God that never fails. We know that we must take the position of LEGACY. That is what was left to us and no one can take it away.

I began this book after experiencing great turmoil and it has taken nearly 10 years to get it out of my head and heart and into your hands. It began in 1998 as I was packing and came across the engraved, crystal acknowledgement of my time at the University of Florida. I was still on probation and feeling the sting of the "Scarlet letter". Now in 2008 a finished manuscript is the key to healing old wounds and laying the demons to rest. *Not for myself but for others* as Mother Dear used to say. I cannot tell our story without remembering hers as we would have no life were it not for the life of Mary.

**I knew her as my grandmother…
What better way?
Evelyn Bethune and Mary**

# *I Leave You*

# *Love*

My very first memory of my grandmother, Mary McLeod Bethune, called Mother Dear by her family, is with my Cousin Georgia in the kitchen of Mother Dear's house. The morning air in the kitchen was always filled with the smell of fried southern ham (bone in), fried eggs and grits with the red gravy from the ham, hot biscuits with real butter and apple jelly. The back door was always open and there was always a place for me and my oldest nephew Donald. Donald is the son of my oldest brother, Albert Bethune, Jr. Albert, Jr. is 30 plus years older than me so I have many nieces and nephews that were born before me. Now, Donald was never mean to me but I guess there is not a whole lot you can say to a three year old over breakfast so we never had any worldly conversations and I was much more interested in biscuits, grits and gravy. I loved the chatter of Mother Dear and Cousin Georgia as they prepared for the day. They never seemed to feel that I was in their way.

At age three, I was still sucking my bottle and I usually arrived with bottle in hand and curiosity on my mind. I loved to sit under the table in the kitchen or in the office under Mother Dear's gigantic desk. Now some of you may be wondering why a three year old would still be sucking a baby bottle. Well... Thank God my mother was not into child psychology and did not feel that I would suffer brain damage or have a warped personality if allowed to suck my bottle until I got ready to stop. Although looking back on some of my early adult behavior, she may have been mistaken. However, I was about 5 years old when I decided to give up the bottle. By now, I was fixing it myself and I think I liked it because I could drink my juice lying down and not spill it on my clothes. I never took it to nursery school, but once I got home, it was me and my bottle. The summer that I gave up my bottle, we were going on a train ride to Philadelphia, and I did not want to be seen on the train with it, so I threw it in the woods next to our house. We were in Philly about two weeks and I never asked for that bottle. Immediately upon returning to Daytona however, I requested my bottle and mommy said, "If you want it you'll have to go into the woods and get it." I immediately gave it up and moved on to drinking out of a cup. I recount this simply to give you an idea of just how precocious I was at an early age. At the age of 3 I was making the trip to Mother Dear's house pretty much on my own. Mommy would stand in the door of our house and watched me as I crossed the street to Mother Dear's house. We all lived within shouting distance of each other.

About a month after my third birthday party, I can remember the bells on the campus of Bethune-Cookman College tolling in recognition of Mother Dear's death and the feeling of sadness in our house for a very long time. For days after the tolling of the bells, there were many people in our house. The coming and going, early and late went on for a time and then stopped. On one particular day there was great story telling by those who came and I remember sitting on my daddy's lap as he talked about the building of Bethune-Cookman from a one room shack to the institution left by his mother. He had many stories to tell about his life as the only child of the great Mary McLeod Bethune. My father was born on February 3, 1899, in Sumter, South

Carolina to Albertus and Mary Bethune. Daddy spent fifty-six years of his life helping his mother build her dream, sometimes deferring or giving up his own. He was in partnership with one of the greatest Americans who ever lived. Many say that my grandmother helped shape the life of Black people in America during one of the most critical periods in our history. I choose to say that she shaped life for Americans as a whole and helped all she encountered to be better than they were before they met her.

When Mother Dear started the mission school in Palatka, FL, my father was there. When she moved to Daytona Beach to start yet another school, daddy was there. In "The College Built on Prayer" it states that Mary McLeod Bethune began what is now Bethune-Cookman University, with one dollar and fifty cents, five little girls and faith in God. The truth is that she started with a dollar and fifty cents, five little girls, one little boy (her son and our daddy), and a *mighty* faith in God. My father's initial education began in the one room school house in which Mother Dear taught. Mother Dear would later send him to boarding school with Lucy Laney in Savannah Ga. Anyone who had a desire to learn was welcomed at these mission schools that my grandmother and women like her began. These were not land grant schools started by whites who did not want their children in school with black children but in many cases were started by churches like the Presbyterian Church that helped Mary Jane McLeod begin her education. She had an insatiable thirst for education and an unstoppable drive to share what she learned with others. She knew that education was the real key to freedom for a people still wearing the shackles of discrimination, segregation and institutionalized racism.

My grandmother's story is a powerful story that needs to be repeated over and over again, because the strength that comes from knowing her never fades. In my darkest moments I was able to find God by remembering my grandmother.

When I was born, my father was 53 years old, he already had an adult son, Albert Bethune, Jr., whom Mother Dear adopted because my dad was not married to his mother who was Caucasian. She was also a citizen of the Bahamas and Mother Dear did not want to risk Albert Jr. being taken away. It was not acceptable in those days to bear children out of wedlock and this was her way of making sure that Jr. was seen as a legitimate member of her family, and not an outsider. Albert, Jr. was an only child for 30 plus years and in many instances resented having to share that space of "grandchild" with his siblings. On many occasions he has denied even having any brothers and sisters going so far as to tell people that our mother already had "those children" when she married our daddy. During his early life Albert, Jr. lived a life filled with whatever he felt he wanted. He lived what he calls the "Life of Riley'. The meaning of the phrase is to have an easy and pleasant life.

Our grandmother ensured that he received an excellent education from Morehouse in Atlanta and that his family was cared for even when he was irresponsible. Junior, as I affectionately refer to him was married a couple of times prior to his current marriage to Lady Marion and borne to him were 11 children. His oldest son, Donald was born out of wed lock and was loved by Mother Dear, cousin's Georgia, and Lucille. But Albert, Jr., on the other hand, had very little time for any of his children until Christopher was born. Christopher is the last child and is a bright, intelligent and warm individual. I am glad to call him nephew. Christopher received all the love and care that Jr. did not have time for with his other children. This lack of fatherly nurturing and basically a disconnection from all family responsibilities as the eldest grandchild produced a void that is still felt throughout our family today. Because there was such a big difference in our ages when Mother Dear passed away, Jr. was appointed to ensure that the family connection to the college and other institutions started by our grandmother stayed intact. Instead, he reaped the benefits of "star-status' and did none of the work for maintenance. By his own description, he was caught up in "chasing women" and enjoying the life of a single man, except for the fact that he was MWC, married with children. When I was born, Jr. already had Donald, Albert III, Samuel, and Patricia. Michael was born after me, and then came Mary, Charles and Sterrly. The seven born after Donald were from his second wife, Betty Virginia Jones Bethune. Betty is and was one of the hardest working women I ever encountered. She managed to get her college degree while married to my brother and having seven children by him. She came into their marriage with a son, named Willie Leonard, so she truly knew how critical it was for her to get her degree so she could take care of her children. My brother was no help; even though he was very well employed by the college as a Librarian, most of his time and money was spent elsewhere. His children were primarily provided for by our grandmother, Mary McLeod Bethune, our daddy Albert, Sr., his step mother, Elizabeth and Betty's parents. It is the same Elizabeth that took care of him as he suffered with sickness due to his heavy drinking.

My mother, Elizabeth (Beth) Sterricks Bethune, was twenty years younger than my father but the love they shared was epic. My mother often told us how "Madame Bethune" initially was not in favor of her son, Albert, Sr., being involved with her, after all, she was a high school drop out, leaving school in the 12th grade to get married and give birth to my oldest sister, Theodora. She was also a divorcee, living in the projects with what many would have viewed as a lower social standing than many of the socialites vying for his attention. Time however would change the mind of Mary McLeod Bethune because other than God there was nothing she loved more than her family.

Mother Dear shaped the lives of thousands before her death in 1955 and institutions established by her continue yet today. The National Council of Negro Women is one of the most outstanding international organizations for training women in leadership and networking in the country. Bethune-Cookman University, under the leadership of Dr. Trudie Kibbie Reed is one of the fastest growing, financially stable, Historically Black Universities in the country, still providing one of the best liberal arts educations for a private institution of higher learning anywhere. These are just two of the institutions that she founded and there are so many more that she touched by adding her remarkable organizational skills to their development. Organizations such as the NAACP, the organizing body for the United Nations, the American Red Cross, these were made better and stronger because of her input. What set her apart? What gave her strength to move mountains of racism and open doors in the arenas of education, the Federal Government, Economic development and Community organizing? When it seemed the most impossible, she did her best work. Her faith was unceasing and her willingness to serve others unquestionable.

Our family almost allowed "the system" to make us believe that our ancestry did not matter and that no one owed us anything. For a long time we felt like we should just walk away from the legacy left by our grandmother because those she left as stewards to care for it chose to exclude her family. On the road of life there are many pot holes and ditches; these are places for you to fall into if you're not careful and especially if there is no one to guide you. We made mistakes for sure as that is part of life. The greatest mistake made by the stewards was not making a place at the table which was built with the blood, sweat and tears of my grandmother, especially for those she left in their care, her family and in particular, her grand and great grand children. Too much effort was put into saying to little children that you are not welcomed here for it to have been an accident or an oversight. But then God...

God has a way of making the crooked road straight, picking up the shattered pieces of your life and making it whole again. This doesn't mean you will never make another mistakes; it just means that you know to never ever give up.

The story of our family is a story anchored in the strength of ancestral Africans who did not give up, and in their struggle, gave us strength. They marked our DNA so that strength would be passed from generation to generation; even today this legacy continues.

When I speak to Black people in the United States who have traveled to the mother land, the continent of Africa, without exception the same phrase emerges... "Life changing". It's life changing to connect with that piece that has been missing; life changing to feel what the ancestors felt when snatched away from all they knew and loved; life changing to be in what we think of as a foreign land and see people who look like your Big Mama and Uncle Rufus; life changing when many times they say to you, ... "Welcome Home!"

For me, this book is my *Welcome Home* to my brothers and sisters, my nieces and nephews, my little cousins, my daughters and especially my grandson, CJ. What an injustice if I ignored this opportunity to speak from my side and talk about the beauty, the heartache, of growing up Bethune.

There have been times in my life that I deeply regretted the choices that I made. I used to believe that the only person I hurt by doing this was myself. I have come to fully understand this is not true. Even when I was very naive or when I felt that nothing I did mattered, or that I must heal the world at my own expense in order to be worthy, or when I got caught up in bad behavior or bad relationships because I was angry or hurting, the end result was the same. We always hurt the ones we love and the ones who love us. We must learn early to "stop, look, and listen, *BEFORE* we cross the street".

It is my belief that God always gives us a sign when we are headed in the wrong direction, we simply choose to ignore that uneasy feeling because it is something we really want. We work it out in our heads. I am sure that when my brothers were told to get off the campus, they were not welcomed there, something did not feel right to the person saying it, but they worked it out because they were repeating what they had been told to say, but for them it was only a job. For my brothers it was like someone spitting on them and they didn't understand why. It adversely affected the way they felt about a place that to us, will always be sacred ground. Our grandmother is buried there.

> They sharpen their **tongue**s
> like swords and aim their
> words like deadly arrows.
>
> Psalms 64:3

I am often asked…"What is it like growing up the grandchild of the famous Dr. Mary McLeod Bethune?" The answer for me is always the same. "It is work, hard work". There is a level of responsibility that comes with this kind of legacy left by my grandmother. The heritage, the ancestry; both have great meaning. Her life has made a profound impact on those of the past; certainly on the present, even future generations will benefit from what she's contributed to humankind. It is not to be taken lightly, or handled carelessly. I say all of this in hindsight, because as a child, I had no idea what it meant to be the granddaughter of one so great, in the eyes of so many, and there was no handbook on how to travel this road.

Dr. Mary Jane McLeod Bethune accomplished more in her lifetime than would ever have been expected. She was conceived of Africans who were once enslaved in this country. Mary Jane McLeod was the product of greatness, a link to the royalty never to be visited again in the home land of her parents. My great grandparents endured the degradation of enslavement, without losing their strength of character, the dignity of their lineage, and their great ancestral love for family … thus the story begins.

# In the Beginning...

Love is a force we must not take lightly.  It is the thread that binds the universe, gives life and brings about the truly miraculous.  Love moved God to create this world, and to breathe His life into man.  It was love that guided three kings from the East to a baby wrapped in swaddling clothes in the Jewish town of Bethlehem; led only by a star in the sky.  And it was the greatest love that gave Jesus the strength to endure the painful death of crucifixion; to give life through the resurrection.  Love is by far the most powerful force on earth.

During some of the worst events in the history of mankind, love kept faith and hope from falling away.  I have often wondered how the enslaved African people of my ancestry could keep going as they did. Their situation seemed beyond hopeless.  The people of the African Holocaust were not allowed even the basics of maintaining our culture, languages, music, or the passing of ancestral history. All links to the varied cultures of our past were stripped away, replaced by a system determined to dehumanize these strong and capable people.

The stolen ones were not the weakest but the best of the best, skilled and intelligent, strong in mind, body and spirit. These Africans were taken from their land, against their will, separated from family and culture, yet still remained connected by their spiritual beliefs. This connection of spirit is what I believe, allowed our people to live, to survive, in spite of the harshness of enslavement.

They had love; love of a land and culture they could only touch in their dreams; love of a people they could only feel in their hearts; love of a distant memory that grew more faint with the passing of time, yet the essence still lingers; it is in our cultural DNA.

My grandmother would hold on to these truths; she understood the importance of having a fervent respect and love for Almighty God. This was something that was instilled in her early on in life; even as a child. This love for God was born into her. Her faith would become her rock, the source of her wisdom and strength.  Some lessons cannot be learned from any mountain of books. Mary knew how to love God because it was something she witnessed everyday.  We learn most effectively through example. The example for Mary Jane McLeod was her parents. Her father's name was Samuel, and her mother's name was Patsy. She remembers her grand mother and the incredible strength of this African Queen. Her sixteen brothers and sisters also gave power to the word family because most of them were born before her and enslaved, yet they stayed connected to home in the worst of times. Mary could also count on the loving support from a community that was there for each other through the worst of times.

Samuel and Patsy McLeod came out of their enslavement alive, mentally sound, and still connected in mind, and body; which was amazing in itself. (Glory to God) Their faith also survived and would make them strong as ever.  It would have been so easy to blame God for what they had endured.  Several of their fifteen children had been sold to nearby plantations as enslaved Africans; how was it possible for Patsy to face each morning and not fall into hopelessness? How could she continue to resist thoughts that God had forsaken her? *This is the day that the Lord has made and I will rejoice and be glad in it.* To truly know and love God is to be infused with His strength. Patsy loved God, and somehow she knew that life would not always be filled with grief, or the sadness that comes in watching the sale of your children with no power to stop it. How do I know this? I know because the strength of that faith was placed inside my grandmother and she passed it on to my daddy who in turn gave it to us.

I do not strive for greatness because of who Mary Jane McLeod Bethune is to the world. I have always desired to achieve because of who she is to my family. Her blood is my blood, and that strength within her also flows in me. I excel because it is in my nature to do so, it is in my blood; it is a part of my cultural DNA. I have faltered, I have stumbled and I have sometimes fallen on my face but I always knew to call on the name of Jesus. I can never remember a time that I did not believe in God; even when I did not believe in myself. There was always something in my spirit that kept me close to God.

The greatest legacy of my grandmother is her great faith in God. He was her source of strength and the one who would guide her through her darkest times in history. One of the greatest legacies you can leave to your family and those who knew you is a love legacy. It is a legacy which shows you that you were sincere in loving God and in loving them. This is what Samuel and Patsy taught their children, and it is exactly what my grandmother taught me.

For a very long time, like Peter, I tried to deny the legacy that my grandmother left us, mistakenly thinking that it resided in the material trappings of buildings or currency. I felt that because our family was systematically separated from the visual legacy that carried our name, we were also separated from all that connected us to our ancestors. But GOD has a way of making it plain.

In order to tell the story of Mary and her grandbabies it is necessary to first tell the stories told about how Mary came to be, the strength that brought her forward. Today we spend a great deal of time and money researching why our communities, the black communities, are in crisis. We want to figure out where we went wrong and why we have made no progress of any magnitude as a community in over 400 years of struggle. It is my belief that we must remember where we come from and who brought us if we are going to fix what is broken. The media, the "system" all tell us that Black people are generationally bad, dysfunctional, genetically predisposed to lower intellectual achievement than others, especially Caucasians. We have spent a great deal of time swallowing that mess and then wondering why we are dying mentally and physically at a faster rate than anyone else on the planet.

Les Brown says, "Garbage in, garbage stays". The negative we ingest mentally, feeds the pariah of bad behavior. When our young people feel that they get more cool points from going to jail than from going to college, it is the parents that need to be checked not the system. My grandmother was able to come out of the darkest of places into the light because of who was holding the lantern. The story of my great grandparents is a story of love and strength that is anchored in the mother land of Africa and cannot be separated from its roots no matter how wide the ocean. I must call the names of Samuel McLeod and Patsy McIntosh so that they may also be remembered in this memoir of BETHUNE.

## Samuel and Patsy McLeod
## Father and Mother of Dr. Mary McLeod

## Samuel McLeod and Patsy McIntosh

As Patsy McIntosh was awakened from sleep, opening her eyes she noticed the dew covered morning. She also realized there weren't any maids busting about her tiny makeshift bed. Her wedding attire had not been created from the finest yards of satin shipped directly from Paris. Her bouquet would be a handful of freshly picked wildflowers from the field, and maybe a thin strand of jasmine, in place of a veil on her head. There was neither a decorated church, nor a lavish reception awaiting this bride and groom. The day would be far simpler than the festivities that could often be heard from the master's stately plantation house.

I can only imagine the smile that must have spread across her face as her eyes slowly grew accustomed to the dim light of early morning. How much more wonderful could any other day be than this delightful morning that would bind Patsy to the man she loved? She was like Rachel and her Samuel was like Jacob. We know that Jacob worked for years so that he could wed his beautiful Rachel. In like manner Samuel toiled over and above what was required to earn the payment necessary to bring Patsy to his plantation. It's important that we understand that my great granddaddy made a deal and kept it; now the blessings of God, and the ancestors could not be denied.

Mary Jane McLeod would spend her Saturday afternoons telling the stories of life before greatness. She would expose unto a spirit of determination possessed by Samuel, and she would tell us about Patsy's unique spirit of. She had story hour with her grand and great-grand; including other children from the community. We called her Mother Dear (*Mu Dear*) because she loved, and cared for us so much. I can still hear the tenderness and life in my grandmother's voice as if I were still a small child, listening to the passing down of oral family history. This was the history of the beginnings of our *"Africans In America"* story. We were too young to know it then but we would learn to appreciate it all the more as we grew older.

Samuel and Patsy's wedding would take place on a piece of land just outside of Maysville, South Carolina, a tiny rural area filled with small, family owned plantations that grew tobacco and cotton. Today, the beauty of the land remains vivid in the richness of the soil and the strength of the people who still work the land. Hollywood has often portrayed the South as a utopian world; thick green curtains of low hanging willow trees were a stark contrast to the bustling cities and factories in the northern states. They really were not so inaccurate in their description of what God created. Cool winds across acres of rolling fields felt like a feather caressing your cheek. The night sky was an expansive canvas to display God's handiwork to everyone on earth.

My grandmother also spoke of a hard life for those trying to plow an existence out of land in Maysville that they had been made to work for free and even after the Emancipation; they had little to grow upon. In those reflections lived the memory of her grandmother, whose body bore the evidence of the enslavers lash with scars that raised themselves to be visible to the eye as a reminder of the true price of freedom. My great-great grandmother was a woman of medium height, dark brown, glowing skin and heavy gray locks of hair. In an interview with Mr. Williams, Mother Dear said that her grandmother had keen features and sparkling eyes with a "very decided voice. There was great feeling of mellowness in her tones and what she said showed signs of great suffering. But she experienced great hopes for those of us that were coming up. My mother was full of hope and faith; she was a triumphant person." This great grandmother of ours told how she was whipped by her masters at her refusal to perform many of the requests made of her brought many stripes to her back. Mother Dear said that the *"subduing of my grandmother's body, the yielding of herself would not come easily."* She said how proud she was that her Mary was not a slave and would not have to pass through the kind of suffering that she had to pass through. She told her that someday she would be a great woman and bring great happiness to her father and mother. She said that in order for Mother dear to be who she was, it was necessary for great grandmother to endure great suffering.

Mary McLeod said of her grandmother *"she exalted me to hold and cling to that which was right and honorable and true in womanhood. Because of her refusal to become subjected to the indulgences of her master, but thank God those stripes would never have to be placed upon me!"* My great grandmother worked in the fields for long hours, whether it was hot or cold, it did not matter. I am certain she rejoiced when Emancipation was declared.

The steady creaking of Mother Dear's rocking chair on her front porch became music to my little ears. She spoke almost wistfully of the first time her father ever laid eyes on her mother. He was instantly smitten with the sweet and demure Patsy. Samuel was visiting the McIntosh plantation with master McLeod. "These wonderful African people used to have these interesting parties; parties to strip fodder and huge parties to pick cotton. Some neighbor would need to get a certain amount of cotton picked and baled by a certain time and they would ask other land owners to help out with the labor. The enslaved would come from miles and miles around and they would pick hundreds and hundreds of pounds of cotton in one night. The next day that cotton would be taken to the gins and mills for sale. It was at one of these *cotton picking parties* that my mother and father met. Their eyes met as they worked side by side and Samuel just knew he was going to marry that bright smiling woman who walked like she owned the world instead of it owning her and held her head high, like the queen she knew herself to be."

It was not uncommon for the enslaved Africans to enter into a bond of marriage and try to raise a family, though many times it was not a recognized ritual or condoned by the plantation owners. This ritual of marriage was seen as a way to placate the enslaved so that they were easier to manage. Since these Africans were considered the property of their masters, there was always a fear within the families that any children would be taken and sold. But love is greater than fear, and they continued to grow and add to their families. The desire to mate and reproduce has been present in man since they were placed in the Garden of Eden by God. What was much less common was how Samuel and Patsy came to celebrate their wedding day. Every time I think of this story I am reminded of the awesome power of God to move mountains and the determination of my great-grand father to marry and uphold the rites of passage that he knew held the blessings of God on his family. Love is a very powerful and very unstoppable force.

Something inside Samuel decided long before he fell in love with Patsy McIntosh that he was going to work at doing his best. My great grandfather, Samuel, believed that even though his body might be held captive, his mind and spirit belonged to God. It was Godly character that had already been established inside this man, and eventually brought him respect among the other Africans and even with the plantation owner. Many times it is mistakenly believed that the captives brought from Africa were without spiritual faith, but though they may not have been attached to the European concept of "Christianity", they truly knew the favor of God and were connected to the Creator of all things long before there was a word called religion. Samuel was driven by his connection to his people, his ancestors and his God. He would do his best, no matter how difficult, and in his own quiet way, he persevered.

Samuel's circumstances were much like Joseph in the Bible. Joseph was a Hebrew slave in ancient Egypt who worked his way up to one of the most powerful positions in the kingdom, second only to the Pharaoh himself. Samuel

McLeod walked in enough favor that his owner often hand-picked him to assist on outings to town and to other plantations. Did his master notice his happy disposition and inquire of the reason, probably not? Somehow Samuel was able to return and spend time with the object of his affection on other occasions.

The obvious obstacles of their budding romance were distance and enslavement by two different men. Master McIntosh did not care much about the emotional well being of his enslaved Africans, so he did not give any consideration to the young couple's plight. But the hand of God was moving. He was softening Master McLeod's heart towards Samuel and Patsy. McLeod worked out a deal with both Samuel and with Master McIntosh; extra work on Samuel's part would earn enough credit to purchase Patsy from her owner. McIntosh agreed to sell Patsy, but only if she was allowed to come to the McIntosh Plantation 2 or 3 times a week to work in the kitchen and laundry. The deal was made and God's plan was set.

The Bible says that Jacob worked for a period of seven years in order to have Rachel given to him as his wife. Because of his love for her, the years passed like days for Jacob. Two years passed from the time Samuel's owner brokered the deal with him to the day that Patsy and his children arrived at the McLeod plantation. Those months, though filled with long hours and great difficulties, must have passed by as mere minutes in Samuel's heart. That kind of love is what builds strength; even in the midst of challenges brought on by enslavement. Samuel and

Patsy may have been alone for many nights, but they were never lonely. Their love anchored them and their family. It helped to sustain them when all they had was faith, love and each other.

There was an even greater joy that splendid morning for Samuel and Patsy; they were not only uniting themselves, but their little family would finally be together as well. Two sons had been conceived and born from the love Patsy and Samuel shared for each other. She would continue to work for her former owner as a part of the deal that was decided between the two plantation owners, but home would now be with her husband and children. They were going to be a real family now or at least for a while. Though Samuel and Patsy were only in their teens when they began their family, they would have a long life together rearing seventeen children. It is important to say that these seventeen children were full sisters and brothers and that they stuck together through all kinds of difficulties, many of them through the Civil War. It was the hand of God that allowed them to remain connected. Samuel was eighty-four at his death and Patsy eighty-three. Samuel died before Patsy.

History does not record much of my great-grandparents, only of my grandmother Mary Jane McLeod Bethune. I find it interesting that so little is mentioned of her roots as it was her parents who gave Mother Dear the foundation on which she built her life and dreams. Her personality and natural characteristics were passed through their blood, and is a map of her past and heritage. Would

Mother Dear have accomplished any of the feats for which history remembers and celebrates her, if Samuel and Patsy had not been her parents?

Samuel and Patsy McLeod took pride in their independence and competence in the performance of their duties before and after the end of slavery in 1865. Patsy worked in the kitchen at the McIntosh plantation. She was also a nanny for her owner's children. Samuel was a man of few words and many talents. He was a very skilled blacksmith, and seemed to have a green thumb in the field. Samuel made a deal with his enslaver to put in extra time and provide services to other plantations that would bring money to McLeod, if McLeod would purchase Patsy so that they could be married. McLeod agreed to this deal. It was the work of at least five men that he took upon his already tired shoulders to earn the purchase of Patsy. But God had His hand on Samuel.

The book of Isaiah says that we can exchange our human might with that of our Father. We can "mount up on wings as eagles" and renew our strength. I am sure the spirit of God surged through my great-grandfather and held him steady; the warmth of that holy presence soothing his aching muscles. God blessed every seed that Samuel planted. What other men may have seen as luck or good fortune, he knew it was the favor of God the Father.

Samuel and Patsy made a very attractive couple. They both had eyes like a sea of chocolate that saw the world in a new light of hope and life. Samuel was almost six feet tall, and must have towered over his bride. He had a ruddy brown complexion and ruggedly strong hands. Regardless of how much labor had roughed his skin, I imagine they felt like velvet the first time Samuel lifted his fingers to trace over Patsy's cheek. Even his deep, rich voice complemented her softer tone.

The wedding celebrations that were held by the enslaved Africans were quite different from the splendid and frilly affairs that southerners richly catered to. There is one particular ritual known as "jumping the broom" that many historians speculate was widely used by enslaved Africans before and after their arrival in North America. This hints to the possibility that at least one morsel of our culture survived the transplant.

Although it may very well be an ancestral tradition from Africa, "jumping the broom" is most certainly a family tradition. And it began on that marvelous day. This was an exciting moment for Samuel and Patsy; that seemingly small action signified the sealing of a lifelong covenant. It was a happy time for the new McLeod family.

Samuel had been preparing for this day for what must have seemed like a lifetime. I can imagine that great granddaddy's heart ached every time he had to leave my great grandmother and their boys at the McIntosh plantation. It was two years of visiting back and forth and though married in spirit and raising children, their desire to be in a home together never diminished. Patsy was a strong woman and the years of living on different plantations and rearing their children with Samuel away much of the time did not bother her heart because she knew that Samuel was her husband and she was his wife. She prepared for the time when they would share a home. As Samuel worked, Patsy also did her part. She was passed to owner Ben Wilson when he married the daughter of McIntosh and as she worked diligently for this family, Wilson, deeded Patsy five acres of land. It was on this land that Samuel would build a log cabin for his family. As the years passed he would build a sturdier cabin with logs cut by he and his sons.  It may not have resembled the sprawling mansions that sprinkled the southern landscape, but the small homestead was a castle in the eyes of his wife and children. The love in that robust little house was a warm embrace to anyone who crossed the threshold. Through the years the family grew, and later freedom became more than a fading memory but a real possibility as the South felt the pressure to *'let my people go'*. As the talk of war increased I am sure my great grand parents thought of how this would affect their family, many of their children had been sold to neighboring plantations. How my great grandfather must have grieved each time he was unable to save his children from the auction block. *"Oh Pharaoh, let my people go"*.

For many months there was tension, steeped as the rumors of impending war, were steadily mounting across the still fledgling country.  Congressional sessions began resembling bar room brawls than dignified discussions. The simmering emotions between the North and the South were quickly becoming much like a steaming volcano ready to erupt.  The issue of slavery had created a great divide between those who supported the right of all men to live free, and those whose affluent livelihood was very dependent on the enslavement of others.

These debates were the same as they had always been, with no one willing to compromise; but suddenly new words were being introduced into these old arguments that brought much doubt to the solid unity of America. News of a possible cessation from the Union by the southern states was bound to make its way into the fields. The enslaved Africans though uncertain of what the future held, prayed and planned for the day freedom would come knocking. You see, many of the Africans knew that it was better to live free in uncertainty than in bondage on the guarantee of degradation

Unbeknownst to anyone at the time, God had strategically placed Patsy in a position to garner important information in order to keep her family and community updated. She would pray for the safety of her family and for the country. In 1861 eleven states in the South formally left the United States and formed the Confederacy under Jefferson Davis.

A good number of years had passed for Samuel and Patsy McLeod since their wedding day. Ten more children filled their small cabin to the brim, fashioning a plethora of memories and experiences. This McLeod Family did not have much but they had more than most of their friends. Samuel and Patsy also had faith that they would come through the worst of it intact, and so it was.

Even in the face of loss, when owner McLeod decided to sell several of their children, the family unit stayed strong. Their faith and love in God did not waver. Nor did their love for one another; it only grew stronger with each passing day. The Civil War waged on for almost four devastating years. Many enslaved Africans were pulled from their duties and families and made to fight for the very thing they despised.

In the end, much of the once decadent South was in ruins and slavery was officially abolished by President Lincoln with the signing of the fifteenth amendment. He did not do it because it was the right thing to do but in lieu of the economic impact of cessation on the country. It was a time of renewed hope for thousands of African. They were free, but what did that mean?

Patsy and Samuel managed to stay in touch with most of their children and when the war ended, they were able to reassemble on the old McLeod place. For some of the children, it took longer but eventually they all managed to get back home to Samuel and Patsy,

Through the favor of God, Samuel and Patsy still had the land that would be used in the future to feed and care for the family. In many ways the outcome of the Civil War did not dramatically alter their lives which included the children. As their children returned with husbands and wives of their own, Patsy and Samuel found that they had grandchildren that they had never seen, as with numerous other former enslaved Africans, Patsy continued to do the same job as always that now included a meager wage. Samuel became one of McLeod's many share croppers. He was able to continue farming his plot of land for personal use, and received seed and supplies from his former owner for commercial crops. The money earned was a paltry sum, but it was a start for Samuel. Those working the land never seemed to get ahead of those who controlled the seed and the fertilizer but *free* was still better no matter the circumstances. Even when the promise of "forty acres and a mule" was not kept...*FREE* was still better.

Housing conditions did not improve, and provisions were not in abundance for so many in the southern states. Antebellum laws in South Carolina forbade enslaved Africans from learning how to read and write. They were also unschooled in simple arithmetic that became necessary when conducting business and shopping for basic necessities. It may have appeared that they were still on the losing end, but despite all of the negatives, Samuel and Patsy were determined to take the blessings from God and keep family and community together.

McLeod now owned the local county store that Samuel and other sharecroppers, black and white frequented. Since none of them knew how to add and properly count, these men had to rely on McLeod to fill their order and keep track of what was owed. When the crops were brought in from the fields to be sold, they also had to depend on him to give them their share of the money. It was a common assumption that the old slave owner did all he could to take advantage of any newly freed

Africans as well as the poor whites who were no better off. This may very well have happened, but the Bible is very clear on the principle of sowing and reaping.

Just as Samuel and his children toiled and planted all day long, their words and actions were just like the seeds they laid in the ground. There is a popular adage that says *what goes around comes around*. This is a basic principle, and no matter what's one religion there is always give and take, reaping what is sowed. The South was bountiful with plantations that do not hold any significant place in the history books. Today, their individual deeds are remembered by no one. These men reaped what they sowed. History no longer mentions men like McLeod and McIntosh except in reference to the lineage and legacy that began with Samuel and Patsy McLeod and is still discussed and celebrated to this day as the life of Dr. Mary McLeod Bethune.

I Leave You

Hope

# Mary Jane McLeod

Every mother knows well the joy of giving birth, and holding their new son or daughter for the very first time. I look at each of my now grown children, and sometimes it feels like just yesterday that I was cuddling their little body in my arms and feeling those ever so tiny fingers grasp mine. Those memories always make me smile. All babies are special, a beautiful masterpiece painted by God Himself. Each of Samuel and Patsy's fourteen children gave them plenty of cause for celebration. But that hot summer day in July was a different kind of birthing for the couple.

The year was 1875. The United States of America was one year shy of her centennial birthday. It had been nearly a decade since the great Civil War would come crashing to an end. Slavery was effectively abolished, and through the gallant and tireless efforts of Frederick Douglass, African Americans were given the right to vote. Life in South Carolina was very slowly getting better for the McLeod family. They had moved out of the one room cabin and into a large home that included a separate kitchen and living room area. When this baby entered the world on the tenth of July, she entered completely free. Mary Jane McLeod was the first child born to Samuel and Patsy after the signing of the Emancipation Proclamation. She was born free. No longer would my great grandparents have to live with the fear of anyone carting off another child. Or at least if they tried, Samuel felt he could fight back and was prepared to do so.

Have you ever felt like God somehow made a mistake when He placed you on this earth? Perhaps you feel like you should have lived in a different time period, or maybe born into a different family. I think everyone has wished for new parents at some point in their life. I believe that everything happens for a reason; for such a time as this. You are here, at this moment, in this family for a specific purpose. You would not be as successful in the fifteenth century because your gift and talent is needed to touch others now.

Would Mary have still been as effective and accomplished as much in her life if she had been born fourth instead of fifteenth? I absolutely believe, as did my grandmother, that she arrived at her appointed time, and not a day too soon.

God knows what He is doing. Mary Jane McLeod was born during a time when Mr. Douglass was boldly carrying the torch of civil liberties and rights for the newly freed Africans, but eventually a new champion would be needed to continue the race. Mary Jane McLeod held a great destiny within her. The older women who assisted Patsy with the birth said she came out with her eyes wide open. Mary was ready to live from the moment she drew her first real breath. She also did not cry out as most babies do. The women called her an *old soul.* They said she was blessed and wise beyond her years.

Growing up in the South during that time period

was not easy. Mary's father Samuel, and most of her siblings worked as share croppers on the McLeod plantation. Her mother was a house keeper and nanny for her former owner Ben Wilson. The hours were very long and it was often dark before everyone was back under the same roof at the end of the day. It was a hard life, but both Samuel and Patsy were determined to take pride in everything they did. And they would give thanks to God for protecting and providing for their family. He had blessed them in the past, and they knew He would continue to bless them even now.

Racial tensions ran high in the years following the Civil War. Much of the South was in the process of being rebuilt. Union armies occupied many portions of every former Confederate state. The Africans had their freedom but not much more. They still lacked equal stature in the eyes of a majority of whites, Union soldiers included. Remember, most of the abolitionist came from the north but they had to fight against slavery in northern states just as hard as in the south. When I think of what my family endured back then, I am amazed how my grandmother was still able to love the people she encountered. How incredibly difficult was it for Jesus to look at the frothing crowd that was screaming for his death and still have compassion for them? He even prayed with his dying breath that his Father forgive them because they did not know what they were doing.

So how did Mary do it? For one, she was taught how to respect others from her parents. And secondly, it was as if Mary had been given the gift of love; a special anointing to see past the ugliness thrown at her and respond with such pity and compassion as would break the walls down that opposed her. God would use her to peel away the scales of hate that blinded so many people, and remind African Americans that it was time to stand up as children of the Most High.

Mary was only a child the first time she was pitted face to face with racism. As a young girl, maybe 8 or 9, she would accompany her mother to work every day at the Wilson estate and play with the children that Patsy cared for. During the days of slavery, Ben Wilson had married one of the McIntosh daughters and when she began to bear children, Patsy's services to the McIntosh's had been passed on to the Wilson's. After Emancipation Patsy stayed on as their cook and cared for their children just as her own. It was on one of these occasions that Mary came to know that whites felt they were better than blacks, even as children.

My grandmother could recall playing with the Wilson children and a few neighborhood friends that her mother also looked after. They all got along nicely enough, but Mary was beginning to feel the divide that kept her from really being a part of the circle. The day would eventually come that altered her path. She happened to pick up a book in the Wilson daughter's playroom. Mary did not understand any of the gibberish on the pages. She knew they were words, but she could not decipher what anything meant. It was at that time that Mary realized she was illiterate. One of the friends saw her staring at the pages, and immediately snatched it away. She scolded Mary, "nigger put that book down, and you know you can't read". Though the Wilson child had never spoken to Mary this way, she did not defend her either but merely suggested a book with pictures. At that moment, Mary prayed to God to deliver her from her illiteracy. She firmly believed that God would hear her prayer though it was only said in her heart.

Even telling this story I can feel the hurt of the spirit that washed over my grandmother that day. In my humanness I can imagine that I would have wanted to say something mean back, or somehow exact vengeance for those hurtful words. And how sad would I feel to look at the girl I had known and played with almost since birth, and she would neither defend, nor help me because of my skin color. I would have been hurt for sure but even more so, angry at not having control of my own life. My grandmother could have done so many things, but what did she actually do? She prayed. She asked God to make a way, so she could be educated.

In the New Testament, Peter once asked Jesus how many times he had to forgive someone. Jesus answered him with "seventy times seven." In other words, as often as it takes for you to be able to lay that offense down and go on with your life. If you have to lay it back down two or three hundred times, then so be it. I believe my grandmother was able to carry the memory without carrying the hurt. She took that and made something positive happen. She did not wallow in her ignorance, she asked to be educated.

The book of Psalms says that if we delight ourselves in the Lord, He will give us the desires of our heart. It may not always be so easy for adults to cast their cares on God and receive His joy, but for a child like Mary it was second nature. And she was not asking for a big house, fancy clothing, or a room full of new toys.

*"If any of you lacks wisdom, let him ask of God, who gives to all liberally and without reproach, and it will be given him." James 1:5*

There is no doubt in my mind that God would have given Mary anything she asked of Him, including the house and toys. But like Solomon, she desired something more precious than gold and silver. Mary yearned for knowledge and wisdom. And just as He promised in His word, God gave her the desire of her heart.

As Mary was bringing her request before God, He was orchestrating the answer to her prayer miles away in Sumter County. The Presbyterian Church had decided to build schools throughout the South for black children to learn just as the privileged young of white plantation owners. The teacher, Emma Wilson, was a pretty young black woman whom the students called "Miss." Though she was a Negro, she was very fair in complexion, "couldn't tell her from white" but she was determined to give her students what she had.

I have often wondered about the laborers that God directs to help make a vision come to fruition. Sometimes they are remembered, like Barnabas and Timothy who served with the apostle Paul. But other times these helpers are behind the scenes, or nameless when the great deeds are recorded in history. Paul is considered one of the greatest of the apostles; he is the author of thirteen books of the New Testament, was used to bring thousands into the kingdom of God, and credited with building many churches across the known world.

The first Christian sent across his path following his conversion on the road to Damascus was a man named Ananias. The Bible mentions Ananias only once when he prayed for and baptized Paul, but he is no less important because of his seemingly small role. Many of the books and printed works about my grandmother do not even mention the teacher by name. She seems to be forgotten to the world. But God remembered her, as did Mary. Miss Wilson loved God and was faithful to do her part in fulfilling the call that was divinely put on Mary. The humble spirit of Miss Wilson showed on her face as she "always had a smile on her face as she greeted us in the mornings". Mother Dear shared these reflections as she told us stories about her childhood. She often said that the whole world opened up to her when she learned to read.

It is almost funny (and sad) nowadays to listen to children complain about going to school. They beg, plead, and fake illness to get out of having to get up and be present in their classes. They will whine about having to walk to the bus stop every morning; at only eight or nine years old, Mary was walking five miles to, and from school just to be able to learn. Each day she was up and on her way, no matter what the weather was like. She was not going to waste this rare opportunity.

Mary's schooling became a blessing for everyone. She would return home and share with her family and the community, black and white, what she had learned. God made a way for both children, and parents to gain the knowledge they needed to conduct business. Mary did not want anyone to be embarrassed anymore for their lack of understanding.

This precious knowledge was not just for her family, but anyone who thirsted. What a humbling experience it must have been for grown men, both black and white, to ask a child to teach them. I believe my grandmother walked in double anointing; to love, and to teach. She already had the heart of a teacher from such a young age. Mary was able to show her father and other share croppers how to properly count out their harvest. It was not unusual for the sharecroppers to give the paperwork to little Mary to make sure it was correct.

I laugh out loud to think of the surprised expressions that must have appeared on the faces of the previous enslavers like McLeod and McIntosh, when the share croppers showed up with this newfound learned information. It did not take Samuel and the others long to see how their past disadvantages had benefited these rich men; but that time was over. The workers were no longer helpless; the scale had finally leveled, no longer would the buyer be the only one able to read the weight and count the money.

School was a euphoric experience for Mary. She soaked in the life water of every lesson; her ambition would prove valuable. She was motivated to help others around her and being able to offer herself in this way was the icing on the cake. When Samuel and Patsy prayed for the same knowledge that their white owners possessed, I doubt they had any idea the answer to their prayer would be granted through their own child. God had a bigger plan than just educating Mary and her family; He was preparing the means to educate a nation and give voice to a people relegated to a position of poverty and discrimination. Of all the books that Mary imagined being able to read, and all the books she would read in her lifetime, the book she was most excited about was the Bible. One of the things I remember most about Mother Dear was the true enthusiasm she expressed over her faith and her joy in knowing God. She could trace back every accomplishment she ever made to a scripture or passage she read. At such a tender age, Mary McLeod would finally be able to read for herself about the God her parents spoke of and prayed to. Was this the same God she heard of when in the big house with her mother? Because I know personally how faithful and loving God is, it is most certain that He would and did find ways to reveal Himself to my family. Mary truly desired to know God, and the Bible says that when we seek Him we will find Him. She flipped open that Bible and found herself in the book of John.

*"For God so loved the world that He gave His only begotten Son, that whoever believes in Him should not perish but have everlasting life."   John 3:16*

The truth was made known to Mary that day.  God spoke to her little heart and showed His love.  She realized that Jesus died for all people, of all languages and all colors.  This everlasting life was for anyone who wanted it.  That scripture became rhema (living and revealed word) to Mary.  Just as she shared her school lessons, she also would share the word of God with her family and the community.

The Bible says that God will use the foolish things to confound the wise.  This is seen throughout the scriptures, and many places in history.  It seemed very irrational and borderline stupid to Israel's high ranking military and royalty that a young shepherd would be able to defeat a formidable foe like Goliath with a slingshot and some rocks.  But God and David proved them all wrong.  The child of a former slave preaching that Jesus died for all of mankind and not just white people may have sounded very foolish.  This was news that shook many wise minds.

Years were passing very quickly for everyone in the McLeod house.  Two more children would be born to Samuel and Patsy after Mary.  Their other children were already productive and engrossed in their own families.  Life was both hard and content for those who still lived at home.  When she was not in school, Mary was helping her family in the fields.  As a child, I loved school and even today I love learning. My days as a child were filled with play and daydreams as I rode my bike or climbed neighborhood trees. What did my grandmother dream about at night?  Did she ever imagine or even glimpse the far reaching effect of her future influence? She often talked about how different she was from her brothers and sisters. She viewed the world in a way that they never did. She even had different food tastes.  Did Mary ever think she would accomplish so much?  Were her aspirations grand or small?

*"I never permitted myself to become discouraged.  I knew from some spirit within me that a better way was coming by and by."*
*Mary McLeod Bethune*

Mary Jane McLeod was growing up from a delightful girl to a strong and caring young woman. Although she physically resembled her father with her robust features, the inside was all her mother.  She was a natural leader, from school activities to working in the fields at home. People were drawn to her confidant personality and unselfish motives.  Mary truly just wanted to help others. I believe Mother Dear grasped what so many Christians cannot seem to comprehend; that God loved her and wanted the best for her. He was never going to forsake her and abandon her.

God was not the only one who was keeping a close eye on Mary.  Her teacher Miss Wilson had taken a special interest in the bright-eyed little girl who loved to learn from the very first day of school. She watched as Mary worked in the community to garner interest and aid for the school, helped in Sunday school, and created clubs at area plantations. Mary also excelled in speech and debating contests. Oh how she loved to debate! Perhaps she was able to see a small piece of the extraordinary vision that was growing inside of my grandmother.

At 15 or 16 years of age, Mary had received all that the mission school could give and thus, returned to the cotton fields as there was nothing else for her in South Carolina or so she thought. But truly God had plans for her that she could not even imagine.

One October day Miss Wilson and a colleague Mr. Simmons who now taught at the school called upon Samuel and Patsy with some news regarding their daughter. They came to the farm field because they had news that could not wait. Apparently Mr. Simmons had been sending out information of all that was happening at the county school and included some writing done by Mary. This caught the attention of a woman in Colorado, Miss Mary Chrisman, seeking to sponsor a young black girl to continue her education at an all girls school in North Carolina called Scotia Seminary, later known as Barber Scotia College. Mary was to be that girl. Now Miss Chrisman was not a rich philanthropist. She was a working woman who allowed God to use her. She stated that out of her earnings she wanted to pay for the education of a Negro girl *"who would make good if given a chance"*. What a return on an investment. God had not forgotten His daughter, or her prayers to be educated. He was still working on her behalf to give her the most knowledge she could possibly have.

# I Leave You the

# Challenge

# of

# Developing

# Confidence in

# One-another

*"I pulled my cotton
sack off, got down
on my knees,
clasped my hands,
and turned my eyes
upward and
thanked God for the
chance that had
come"*
***Mary McLeod-Bethune***

Mary was thrilled for such a wonderful opportunity to gain more knowledge. There was much preparation before the train ride in October that would take her to North Carolina. This was not only exciting for Mary, but also for the neighborhood and community of people that she had assisted over the years. Everyone was more than willing to pitch in and help in getting all that Mary would need for school. Samuel found a small trunk to carry her clothing and belongings in. A few neighbors knitted stockings, and donated dresses. The weeks flew by for Mary as she anticipated her first train ride.

When the day finally arrived, Mary was greeted with a caravan of well wishers outside of her home. A large group was prepared to travel with the family to Maysville and the train station. There was a flurry of handshakes, hugs, and tears as Mary gave her good-byes and boarded the train. As a parent I know how difficult it can be to see your child step into the world. Patsy held her daughter tight and blessed her, committing her into God's hands. It must have been hard to watch Mary begin the journey of her life, but Samuel and Patsy were overjoyed at the bright future she was heading towards. This was the journey that would give hope to those she left behind.

Even as my grandmother progressed in years, her mind remained as fast and sharp as if she were still a child. And her memory never dulled. She could still clearly recollect her years at Scotia Women's College with fondness and sincerity. It was not an easy time for Mary; she was the farthest away from home that she or anyone in her family had ever been. Everything was so different from her humble cabin back in South Carolina.

Mary was feeling very much like a fish out of water as she arrived on the school grounds. The brick buildings were castles to her young eyes. Her bedroom was neat and beautiful. Each of the covered and made up beds reminded Mary of the fancy rooms in the Wilson and McIntosh plantations. Her first morning was truly an amazing experience. The banquet hall where meals were served was so expansive and stately. Mary laughingly recalled her quandary with the place settings and silverware. But in time, all the rough edges soon fell off, and she was well on her way.

It did not take very long for my grandmother to find her groove at Scotia. She did not have much time to be homesick; she was busy with school activities and volunteering to assist whenever called upon. The other girls confided in her with their problems and difficulties. Mary quickly became known as the *peacemaker*. She was well liked by students and teachers, and when she wasn't in class, she did laundry, and worked in the kitchen as part of her scholarship.

The years at Scotia were very productive and enriching for Mary, both educationally and personally. She found herself being surrounded by many different people; people of different races from all walks of life. Her teachers were mostly educated and refined black and white women. Mary began to realize soon after arriving that she had the drive and learning capacity to be just like them, and even better. She also was a born leader. People flocked to her because she had a spirit of giving and earnestly cared for her new community and the young women with whom she attended school.

Deep in my grandmother's heart was a desire to travel to Africa as a missionary. She was still a young girl when she heard Dr. Bowen speak very passionately of the spiritual plight in Africa and the need for people to go and spread the Gospel. During her season of higher learning, she was working and praying about a plan to make her way to the other side of the world, to Africa. God was still revealing His plan in Mary's heart. All she knew was that she wanted to help her people. Her natural leadership ability gave her eye for detail, a quality she was born with, an inheritance from her mother for sure. Her quiet steadiness was her father's gift. She knew she could make a difference as a Missionary and going to Africa would be the perfect work for her life. In her determination, she was even more inspired in her studies.

Mary's time at Scotia was coming to a close as her graduation neared over the next horizon. Although she missed her family deeply, there was also a drive within Mary to continue striving for knowledge. God remained faithful to Mary by opening a door, and an opportunity for her to attend the Moody Bible Institute in the windy city of Chicago. This was a definite eye opener for Mary to see the treatment of her people in other parts of the country. Racism was real and widespread everywhere. In spite of the harsh weather and the realization that black people were suffering all over the country, Mary's faith told her that she was on the right track to help heal some of the wrongs, and believed that education was the key to this freedom. She knew that enslavement did not have to be a visible shackle but could be imposed by the imprisonment of the mind through illiteracy. I know how heart breaking it is when people are mistreated or they're being denied access to the tools needed to improve one's station in life because of their race. My grandmother was determined not to let anyone make her feel less than the child of God that she knew she was. One of her favorite sayings was, *"I am black, and I am beautiful."*

Mary spent two years at the Moody Bible Institute preparing to be a missionary to the faceless crowds of Africa. She poured over the Bible, studying as if starved for weeks and the pages held her food. Her love and admiration for the word of God and her faith continued to deepen. When the time finally came, Mary excitedly sent her application to the Mission Board in New York City for placement in Africa. The response she received was completely unexpected. There weren't any opportunities for Black missionaries anywhere on the Continent of Africa. Imagine that. Descendents of the stolen Africans were not allowed to go back and minister to those who might be their relatives. This must have really stunned my grandmother; her bubble had just been burst. What was she to do now? Mary did not miss a step. She did what she had always done in times of turmoil and confusion – she prayed.

# I Leave You Faith

# Mary

Mary felt her eyes being redirected to this country she called her own; so many of her people here were in need of both a secular and spiritual education. God moved on her heart to accept a teaching position in Augusta, GA to work under the direction of Ms. Lucy Laney. Ms Laney was the creator of Haines Institute. My grandmother was able to learn from strong, black women throughout her developmental years and the women of Haines Institute were no different. Ms. Laney, Ms. Mamie McCrory, Ms. Jackson, Ms. Irene Smallwood( Bowen), were the life blood of the Institute and gave many years of their lives to teach black people, black children in particular, basic educational skills and to love God. Their faith was unstoppable. My grandmother said that it was that kind of faith, the kind that Abraham had, that built Bethune-Cookman.

Ms. Laney allowed Mother Dear to start a Mission Sunday School. She started with the girls in science class and in her own class and as she recalled, they recruited children from all over the community, in any neighborhood until they had almost a thousand young people, even people from the community who just wanted to learn. That mission school lasted for years, long after Mary McLeod moved to Sumter, South Carolina and beyond.

All Mary could think about was how to lead others to the light of education. She was returning to her home state, but still not quite back to her comfort zone. While growing up, Mary had often found herself in positions of leadership with her siblings and fellow classmates. But being a teacher was something very different and special. Mary was going to be responsible for each and every student in her class. They would also learn that they had a responsibility to her. You see, success requires give and take on both parts. The success of the students did not just depend on how good Mary was at imparting the lessons but it would also depend on the willing spirit of the students to receive what she was freely giving. She wanted them to love learning as much as she did.

It makes me smile to imagine the warm reunion that my grandmother shared with her family upon her return. It had been a very long time to be away from home. There was a multitude of family and neighbors to send her off to Scotia so many years ago; there must have been an equally smiling crowd to greet Mary as she stepped down from the train. As much as she enjoyed catching up, there was not much time for relaxing. Mary was ready for the school year to begin and she wanted to be underway with her preparations.

The door to missions work overseas seemed to have been firmly closed. Mary still desired to help others, but she was already beginning to see how many needed assistance in her own backyard. Mary refused any discouragement that attempted to slither into her heart, and mind. It was man that turned her away, not God the Father. Mary knew from the Bible, and from personal experience, that God could open doors that no amount of human strength would ever be able to close.

Her dreams at night must have really been something to behold.  Mary was finally beginning to see her path through praying and studying the Bible, and realize her place in God's plan.  It was a very good place; a very exciting place for Black woman to be in.  Mary kindly dismissed urging from her sisters to get a husband and settle down.  She had trusted God all of these years to make her way straight and guide her.  It seemed only natural to Mary that she trusts in Him to bring her a mate when the time was right.

*Professional women have a much more difficult time balancing work and family than is commonly supposed. According to High-Achieving Women, 2001, between 33 percent and 43 percent of women are childless at ages 41-55 - only 14 percent of them by choice. The percentages are even higher amongst women of color. In addition, the study found that large numbers of highly qualified mothers opt out of the labor market completely. The result: too many women are forced to sacrifice: either family or career. Only a small proportion of these women feel that it is likely they can "have it all" in terms of career and family but feel that men fare better on this front.*
***Sylvia Ann Hewlett's "Creating a Life"***

Mayesville cabin where Mary Jane McLeod was born
Rachel and Maria McLeod are standing in front of the
family cabin.

## Mary & Albertus

The dating scene has never been much of an oasis for women; we are viewed as the meal or the cook, and neither role is held in the most attractive light. As difficult as it can be in the twenty-first century, it was all the more impossible for a woman like Mary in the late 1800s. The notion of choosing the husband instead of being chosen was probably a very foreign idea for women at that time. Mary was not going to jump on the first offer that came along. She was a highly prized daughter of Samuel and Patsy as well as a fully committed Christian woman, and she wanted nothing but the best that God had for her.

Mary could not help but be a little nervous on the morning of the first day of school. There must have been such a rush of excitement as her students filed into the classroom. Was this how Miss Wilson and her other teachers at Scotia felt? In each of their faces she saw hope and the possibility of a splendid future. She saw herself. There had been some rough edges during Mary's first days at Scotia and the Moody Bible Institute, and there were a few rough edges and blunders as she began her new career as a teacher. But as before, it was not too long before Mary smoothed out and found her own distinctive groove.

Mary had become accustomed to people paying her attention and striking up conversations. She was a natural leader and had a very likeable and easy going personality. She wore her inner strength with much respect and dignity. Mary was working with people in jails, the under privileged and people in the community building Sunday Schools filled with young people. She was also singing in the choir. It was in the choir that she met Albertus Bethune. My brother, Albert, Jr. remembers Mother Dear saying about Albertus that he was a "delightful tenor". He was active in the church and at the time they met, he was a student at Avery Institute in Charleston, South Carolina with about a year left to finish his degree. He later withdrew from school to help his brother Jesse enter school. May and Albertus had a whirlwind courtship and fell in love.

It is a beautiful feeling to be in love. Your heart soars on a daily basis. That dreamy smile on your face never really goes away, and everything suddenly looks so rosy and happy. I learned about that kind of love from observing my parents. Regardless of the hectic schedules they faced on a given day, mommy and daddy shared a connection and a love that everyone around could sense like a warm embrace. I imagine that it was the same for my grandmother and grandfather. Mary was not the kind of person to lose her head over anything. She analyzed and reasoned every problem and decision. She also prayed about her life, her career, and her family. Mary had long since passed the care of finding a husband over to the Lord. She fully trusted her God to bring her the best and most compatible mate. And now here she was with her heart fluttering, and envisioning how life might be as the wife of Albertus. Mary knew that he enjoyed her company, but she was not sure if Albertus shared her feelings.

Albertus was more than just fond of Mary. She was

on his mind throughout every part of the day. It made him smile simply to hear her voice, and he found himself praying for her each morning. Mary was truly in his heart. Albertus wanted to be with her all of the time. He was in love, and he could only hope that Mary loved him too.

My grandfather must have had some sweaty palms when he finally worked up the nerve to present his heart to my grandmother. Maybe his speech faltered a bit as he gazed into her cheerful eyes and poured out his feelings before her. One of my grandmother's best features was always her smile; it was radiant and joyfully infectious. I can imagine how her smile lit up her face as she returned his declaration of love and placed her own heart before him.

Modern dating in any form did not exist during that time period. Couples did not sequester themselves alone, make out in a movie theater, or take weekend jaunts to a cozy Bed and Breakfast. And even if they did, Mary would not. The book of First Thessalonians in the New Testament tells Christians to *"abstain from the very appearance of evil."* In other words, do not be in a situation that may merely hint that you may be in the wrong. But the beauty of Mary was that she was a Christian not a warden. She loved life and made those around her love it. She was quick to laugh out loud and people were drawn to her because of her sense of humor and open spirit. This is what also drew Albertus to her. He just simply loved being around her and felt good when he was in her company. She made him feel good about himself and the plans he had for his own life.

This was what he hoped for in the woman with whom he would spend his life.

Now that Albertus and Mary were aware of the love they had for each other, the next step was to meet the family.  True courtship is scarcely practiced in today's society.  Too many men and women choose to even forgo a traditional wedding with family and friends for eloping to Las Vegas.  Albertus traveled to Maysville to meet Mary's parents and formally ask Samuel for his daughter's hand in marriage.

Samuel and Patsy were quite impressed with the way that Albertus carried himself. He was a fine young man, with fine parentage and family and though his educational background was average, he was creative and loved the business world. He also knew his own mind.

Mary's father believed his fiery daughter needed an equally strong and creative counterpart as a husband. They happily gave Albertus their blessing, and plans for a festive wedding celebration were almost immediately underway. Mary could not have been more excited.  Her sisters took pride and joy in fussing over her as if she were royalty. Mary praised God for this most wonderful blessing.

The day of the wedding was a splendid occasion. Mary could remember listening to her mother describe her own wedding celebration.  Did the birds sing as loudly when her parents were united as one?  Was this day as beautiful and happy?  Patsy assisted her other daughters in readying Mary for the ceremony. Regardless of what she was wearing, Mary felt very much like a queen robed in the world's finest fabrics.

It seemed like the entire town showed up to offer their blessings to the young couple. Mary's family alone included sixteen siblings, their spouses, and over eighty grandchildren combined. Everyone who lived near the McLeods' had been invited to attend. Many of the older share croppers were happy to see the once little girl who brought them knowledge and pride stand as a beautiful woman next to her husband.

Albertus and Mary exchanged their vows and pledged their lives to one another. Then came her family's tradition; Mary was thrilled in her heart as she and Albertus jumped over the broom and sealed their commitment. She was happy and in love, and now married. The rest of the day brought much dancing, singing, and a bounty of delicious food. Mary, Albertus, and the rest of the family celebrated well into the twilight hours.

Married life was a bit of an adjustment for both of the newlyweds, but especially Mary. Her usual routines would have to be adjusted to accommodate another person. She no longer had the luxury to come and go as she pleased; like staying late in her classroom or working over the weekends. Mary's sisters were quick to offer marital advice and chide her for her streak of independence. They even dared suggest that Mary consider cutting back on her teaching duties, and maybe even resign her position in order to be a better housewife to Albertus.

This did not sit well with Mary at all. She loved her husband dearly, but she also loved teaching. It was more than just a job; it was a part of who Mary was. She finally felt as if she was walking out her destiny. Mary knew the voice of God was directing her; she knew the things God had spoken into her heart. She brought these concerns to Albertus, who assured his bride that he understood how much she enjoyed what she did. He would never dream of demanding she give that up.

What's most important to the new Mrs. Bethune was that her husband Albertus loved and trusted God and she knew that he was a man of great faith. Mary dreamed of all they could do together to bring change to the lives of many black people that she knew lacked basic educational skills. She knew in the book of Proverbs that God said His people were destroyed for a lack of knowledge. The greatest destruction faced by these newly freed Africans and anyone else deemed illiterate, was to their livelihood and self esteem. How could you grow and prosper in the world if you were unlearned and illiterate? Mary understood that being unable to read and write did not mean that you were ignorant but the outside world would perceive you that way and stumbling blocks would appear. Mary aspired to do all she could to end this plight for her people, for God's people. She did not plan to stop this work for which God had prepared her, not as long as there was a single breath left in her body.

After their marriage they moved to Savannah, Georgia, where Albertus found business employment. God continued to bless Albertus and Mary as they began their new life as husband and wife. Their modest home was decorated with what Mary could find through her family and friends. It was quite tasteful and inviting; she wanted Albertus to feel warm and comfortable when he arrived home from his work. Anyone who visited must have teased Mary about her endless stacks of books. She could easily open her own library. Mary loved to relay the story of how, as a child, she prayed for God to make a way for her education and He did. Just as He promised and just as she believed he would. She did not believe in wasting a blessing from God so she never ceased to learn. Mary planned to learn until her *cup runneth over*, and pass on all that she knew to others.

There was no denying that Albertus and Mary were very happy together. Before meeting my grandfather, thoughts of marriage and babies did not have much place in the mind of my grandmother. She was so focused on her work and studies. Mother Dear certainly loved children, but she did not allow her thoughts to dwell too long on having a family while she was in school.

Watching her sisters hold and love their own suddenly stirred an aching within Mary. She could also see in her husband's eyes that he hungered to be a father. Mary began to pray, not only for a child, but wisdom for herself and Albertus to be godly parents. She wanted to be sure that their children were raised to love and respect God just as she was. Albertus and Mary lived in Savannah, GA for about sixteen months after being married then moved back to Sumter, S.C. due to the work requirements of Albertus. It was at this time that Mary gave birth to their only child.

On February 3, 1899 Albertus and Mary welcomed a healthy baby boy into their hearts and home. He was named Albert McLeod Bethune after his father, and carried McLeod for his mother. Mary felt her heart might burst from the love surging through her for her son. Her desire to help those less fortunate burned even greater inside her soul and spirit after Albert was born. I cannot help but smile when I think of my father as a baby; so alive and so full of hope and potential. He took after his father in many ways, but his spirit came from Mary. My father Albert McLeod Bethune, Sr. had the same passion for learning as his mother. He also had a great love for music and was blessed with a strong voice with a baritone range. In his later years, the Priest at St. Timothy's Episcopal Church in Daytona Beach would say that he always knew when daddy was not in church because he would miss the wonderful sound of his voice. This was an inheritance that he was more than happy to pass on to his children. I remember sitting on his lap as he read the newspaper every day. We always had several news papers from various parts of the country. I learned to read looking at the daily news from the Chicago Defender, and the Pittsburg Courier. We would read and sing. Daddy also had a strong, steady love for God that he did not talk about much. Instead he showed us by the kindness of his heart. It was not unusual for people to ring our doorbell or knock on our door in the middle of the night, when something was wrong and they needed a phone call made or a paper notarized. Daddy had contacts all over the state and just like his mother he would lend a hand wherever he could.

After a brief sabbatical following the arrival of their son, Mary returned to teaching with renewed zeal and dedication. She had enjoyed the time to bond with her baby, but she also missed her students and the classroom very much. Mary was not only teaching the children writing and arithmetic, but also ministering and imparting the Word of God into their hearts. She was also given opportunities to witness to the parents as well. Mary shared Jesus with everyone she came in contact with. Fear did not hold a place inside her. Samuel and Patsy never encouraged any of their offspring to be afraid. Mary simply did not know how to be in fear, nor did she care to learn. She refused to back away from what she believed God was asking of her.

My grandmother was a woman of great strength but she possessed a humble spirit and took great joy in helping others reach their goals. Her work was seldom about her personal needs. It was a humbling experience for her each time someone thanked her. Many of the parents of the young children she taught were the poorest of the poor. Often she was blessed with crops and services in exchange for tutoring lessons. Albertus and Mary were loved and very respected by those they helped. It was a great thrill for my grandmother to see how, through God, her work was positively affecting the Black community.

The Bethunes continued to do as much as they could until Mary was asked by a visiting minister to bring her skills and talents to Palatka, Florida to oversee a mission school. Excited, she jumped at the opportunity. For the Bethunes this meant leaving behind their family and friends for a place very much outside of their comfort zone. But Mary knew this was of God, and Albertus saw this as an opportunity also. So with Little Albert and her husband, Mary moved to a new frontier to continue the work for which God had prepared her. Though Albertus was not interested in teaching, he did not place any stumbling blocks in Mary's path and supported her work in the community. He knew that he had married a different kind of woman and that she would never be content to just stay at home and be a house wife. She was much too strong willed for that.

Albertus was a business man and he opened a haberdashery store in Palatka. He was able to take care of his family and help Mary when she had community meetings or organized the youth. Though teaching was not his passion, he had a strong desire to see black people succeed. Since Albertus owned a wagon and mules, Mary's husband saw this as an excellent way to support his family. He quit his teaching position and began his own business. The hours were even longer and the work was quite a bit harder. Albertus had to load most of the supplies he was carrying into the wagon by himself. But the pay seemed to make up for the sore muscles and loss of sleep.

Mary had her reservations about the work Albertus

was doing. He spent more time on the road than he did at home. She believed he should remain closer to his family. Albertus, on the other hand, wanted Mary to be the one staying home and tending to little Albert and the house. As he saw it, his new business venture was taking care of their financial needs, so his wife did not need to work. Mary could feel a deep sigh inside her heart. Albertus really did not understand. This had never been about money, but about doing what God had destined for her to do. She only hoped that she would not have to choose between her service to the Lord and her husband.

A Young Mary Jane McLeod
Sumter, SC late 1800s

# I Leave You Respect for the Use of Power

*Then the Lord answered me and said: Write
the vision and make it plain on tablets,
that he may run who reads it. For the vision is
yet for an appointed time; But at the
end it will speak and it will not lie. Though
it tarries, wait for it; because it will
surely come, it will not tarry.  Habakkuk
2:2, 3*

In the book of Habakkuk God instructs His people to not only talk about and meditate on their dreams and inspirations, but to also write them down.  Seeing the words help to remind you of your destiny, and also makes it more real to you and anyone who reads it.  It is important to keep focused during those months or years of preparation. There is a time and season for everything; however long it may seem, your time is coming.  Continuing to observe the vision builds unity within the people.

My grandmother, Mary Jane McLeod Bethune put her hopes and dreams in words.  She loved to read and write and I believe my love for journaling comes from her. She kept journals and letters of her life so that those coming after her would have a path to follow. I believe she was beginning to understand the vision that God had placed inside her from the moment of conception.  Even so, did Mary have any idea that an old garbage dump in Daytona would become the future site to the pristine Bethune-Cookman University campus?

This was nothing short of a miracle for those who witnessed the doors open and obstacles fall from the school's inception.  Mother Dear had an unwavering faith that kept hope alive when the circumstances screamed failure.  The waves may have been crashing all around her, but she did not bow or bend a knee except to pray to God Almighty.  She always knew that God would not fail her because He had shown her very early in her life that He would be the great provider.

Memories of my grandmother are faint but sweet, like the lingering taste of sugar cane fresh from the field in past summers.  She was "Mother Dear or *Mu Dear*" to her family and close friends, and "Madame Bethune" to students and those outside of her close circle.  Mary was so warm and caring that most people would never suspect she was so well known, both nationally and internationally.  She made any person in her presence feel as if they had been friends for years.  This was how her friendship with the Roosevelt women blossomed, especially Eleanor. They were kindred spirits and not blocked by race or any other external differences. When asked what she would like to be remembered for, she answered that she wanted to be remembered as a kind person who cared for others greatly.

The dawn of the twentieth century was still warm and fresh on Mary's face as she continued to teach and minister through the mission school she established in Palatka, Florida.  She and Albertus had been in Palatka for about 5 years and Albert was growing up quickly before her eyes.  Albertus was doing well in his business, though spending more and more time on the road.  Mary's mind was always thinking of how she could be of more service to the many people that she knew still needed a way to have an education. She was listening to the stories about the railroad being built and that many of our people were working on that railroad.

> *"Your word is a lamp to my feet and a light to my path."*
> *Psalms 119:105*

The winds of change were churning slowly in the atmosphere when a new minister, Rev. S. P. Pratt arrived, impressed by the work that Mary had done in Palatka, suggested she come to Daytona and launch a school for the many uneducated Black children.  She gave this new opportunity serious thought because it meant having to uproot her little Albert and talk once again to Albertus about moving. Surprisingly, Albertus was not too disturbed. He knew that he had married a woman that would not to be denied when she was moving on what she believed God was directing. She knew from the Bible that God would direct her path as a righteous and loved child of the Most High.  She prayed and meditated on the scriptures for many days before God lit the way that she was to follow.

It was time to move to the popular Florida vacation spot of Daytona.  She loved her school in Palatka and cherished each of her students.  A replacement teacher would have to be sent to the wood mill town of Palatka to continue the mission school.  It was late September, when Mary packed their things and the family moved to this town of Daytona that would become one of the main stops for the Florida East Coast Railroad.

A new city and a young son must have been daunting for Mary as she prepared to journey further south to sunny Daytona. What made the move even more difficult was that she could be making this jump by herself. Albertus was excited because this was a chance for him to expand his business. Albertus was able to contract with the railroad to transport supplies along the path for the new rails. Increasing his business made it a lot easier to make the move with his family.

On the outside, Daytona was a beautiful city for beautiful people. Vacation spot for the rich and famous on the "World's most famous beach was the way Daytona was advertised. In some writings, Daytona is seen as a "new South city" where there was no race issue. This was not the Daytona that my grandmother met when she arrived. Life was not delicious dinners and privileged dances for everyone. There was another side to this southern gem, a less fortunate and more flawed section of the population. These were the people that Mary was coming to help.

There is a popular religious saying that you may not always no when you are in the will of God, but you always no when you are not. I believe that you also know when you are right on target. Jesus said that His sheep know His voice. We are aware when we are making a good decision, and when we are making a big mistake. We always know. Mary must have felt that confirmation in her spirit the moment she entered the city limits. Nothing and no one would be able to convince her otherwise.

There was certainly a need for preparation time. Mary had quite a "To-Do" list to tackle if she wanted her school to open for the next fall term.  She would pray and plot every move through the direction of God so as not to be overwhelmed and frustrated.  The task ahead would be far from easy, but Mary was determined to finish the plan God put inside her and make this school a reality.  What an amazing feeling to know that her life had a grand and meaningful purpose.

*"Faith is the first factor in a life devoted to service. Without it, nothing is possible. With it, nothing is impossible."*
*Mary McLeod-Bethune*

It was September 1904 when the little McLeod family arrived in Daytona Beach.  Mary's first order of business was to find adequate living quarters.  Fancy homes and estates were available for the right price, and the right skin color.  The choices were fewer and much farther between for a Black woman like Mary with a husband on the road and a small child.  But God was with her; she was blessed to locate a nice place to call home, and a landlord who was more than willing to help Mary with starting her school.  It was now time to gather supplies and find students to teach.

With some aid from the minister who brought her to Daytona, Mary began to advertise to the black neighborhoods on the outskirts of the city. Even without telephones, Blackberries, and computers, news was still able to travel in a speedy manner. Mary's reputation had already preceded her; the daughter of former slaves who would dare to defy the southern caste system and pull her out of hiding in the threshing floor. She was almost a celebrity in the communities of her people.

Regardless of any amount of clout Mary might have garnered up to that point, not everyone was jumping through hoops to sign their children up for school. Some parents did not see the necessity for their children to waste time in school when all they were going to do was work in the paper mills or on the beach in the hotels. This must have been one of the more challenging hurdles that my grandmother encountered throughout her life; people who did not have the faith to hope for change. Though they were dissatisfied with the second rate classification that other men had long since placed on them they did not see a way for change. If her only student was her son Albert, she was still planning to have class time beginning in October. But God…

Mary was a determined as ever and went about the preparation as if she had 100 children lined up and ready to go. As the community watched her prepare, some of the parents caught her fire. She had a small roster of students and her son who helped raise money for the schoolhouse rent of $1.50 by selling sandwiches and baked goods. It was not the most impressive structure, but the small run down shack was just the right size for what Mary was venturing into. She knew how to do more with less and would not be slowed by the trappings, or the lack there of, in a building. Her visions had already revealed to her that she was going to educate thousands and she never doubted for a moment.

Boxes of pencils and pens are a "dime-a-dozen" today; you can find a plethora of school supplies at any supermarket, department store, office supply store, and even thrifty stores. They are so accessible to the point that most of these items are carelessly tossed about and taken for granted. How elated my grandmother would have been to be given actual pencils and paper and pens.

The charred splinters of burned logs were substituted for pencils. Young Albert and the other children crushed elderberries to use as ink. Paper bags and pieces of butcher paper would cut into smaller pieces for writing down lessons, spelling, and math problems. There was also the matter of a desk for Mary and chairs for her classroom. A few crates that were stacked to create a makeshift teacher's desk came straight from the dump. Mary used a piece of upholstery material to cover the unsightliness of the crates. She also made a habit of visiting the city dump and the back alleys of hotels for discarded linens and dishes that could be useful in the school.

*"I became adept in begging for bits of old lumber, bricks and even cement. Salvaging, reconstructing, and making bricks without straw were all part of our training."* Mary McLeod-Bethune

Mary was full of hope and anticipation as October neared. She spent much time in prayer and study of the Bible. This was so much more than just a little school of black girls in a simple shack; it was the initiation of a dream come true for her and God. She must have been on cloud nine for weeks. It was just as delightful to watch her young son express an excited interest in learning, despite his age.

# ENTER TO LEARN – DEPART TO SERVE

It was a grand day on October 4, 1904 as the Daytona Literary and Industrial School for Training Negro Girls opened its doors with a handful of students. How amazing it must have been for those girls; did anyone realize that they were standing on the precipice of such an incredible historic event? I wonder if Mary was very nervous as she opened the day with prayer before diving in to the day's first lessons. What a day that must have been.

There were many who doubted that Mary could carry on for more than a few days. She encountered her share of men and women who tried to discourage her efforts. The most obvious was her husband Albertus, simply by his lack of support and assistance. Sadly, some of the negative criticism and reactions come from our own people. Despite being freed almost forty years earlier, they still carried the mental and physical scars of enslavement; they did not yet remember who they were in the kingdom of God. But my grandmother had that revelation while only a child and it was that supernatural knowledge that kept her going. If everyone had the right to salvation through Christ, they also had the right to learn and be educated.

Mary did not have much to give, but God saw her heart. He blessed her prayers and prospered everything that she put her hand to. Mary taught her girls and her son how to read and write. She taught them simple mathematics and penmanship. She encouraged their interest in history and sciences. Yet woven throughout those lessons were life lessons like "The Golden Rule" ... *Do unto others as you would have them do unto you; or Enter to learn, depart to serve; and Not for myself but for others.* All of these quaint sayings were a part of the daily lessons. Even as a toddler, they were a part of my life and as I got older they became a part of the lives of those I have encountered.

Mary also wanted to instill pride and self assurance in her students. She insisted that they be clean and neat before entering the classroom. The condition of your clothing should not have any bearing on your hygiene or how you carry yourself as an individual. Mary believed that cleanliness was a godly characteristic; it was an outward expression of an inward transformation. She was the example for those she taught and it seemed natural that her physical appearance should speak to herself assuredness.

My grandmother also showed her small group of students how to cook and sew. These skills were as basic a necessity as knowing how to read. Mary wanted to prepare the children, from a young age, to be independent. She could recall making her own dresses while attending Scotia many years ago. Mary also saw the possibility of raising funds for the school by sewing wares and baking goodies. Daytona was also a tourist driven economy with many hotels. Other than the railroad, those hotels and motels were the source of employment for most of the freed Africans and their children.

There is a saying that good news travels fast. Bad news and gossip (in my experience) also have their own speedy momentum. But in the case of Mary Bethune and her school, it was most certainly good news. The Bible says, the Word of God does not return void. When you pray and believe and stand fast to your confession, you will see amazing things happen. I know, without a shadow of a doubt, that my grandmother did just that. I know this because her school prospered. It was growing throughout the school term. Mary was not about to turn away any child who desired an education.

The good news of what was happening in a small ragged shack on the "colored" side of town spread quickly. Mary was delighted by all of the positive support she began receiving from the community. Much of the support she received did not come from the "church folks' but from the gamblers and "honky tonk" owners who valued education and wanted a better life for their children and their people. While some black folks remained stubborn and resistant to change, there were some who softened their hearts and lowered their pride to ask Mary to teach them also. Mary knew that change was difficult because it required that you trust the unknown. Faith was required. She had more than her share and she didn't mind giving you some if you needed it. She took full advantage of these opportunities to share Jesus. She was a missionary who never left her (own) country.

The number of students was steadily growing and Mary knew the cottage would be too small by the following October. She was quietly searching the area for another building in which to house her school. Whether it really was all that was available or simply all that was going to be available to a black woman, the only space Mary could find for the school was located at the garbage dump; appropriately dubbed "Hell's Hole". I can just imagine the smells that emanated from that entire area. Despite what anyone else saw, my grandmother saw unending potential; maybe she closed her eyes and imagined stately buildings and scores of young African American students milling about. She was looking through the mind of her heavenly

Father.

The asking price for this landfill was to anyone else an astounding $250. To Mary it was another opportunity for God to prove His might and show how good He truly is. She convinced the owner to accept a down payment of five dollars now and she would give him the balance over a period of two years.

There is someone who once said, "The gospel is free; the wagon train to take it to the world is not." This is the same for education. The knowledge itself does not cost anything, but how you learn does. Mary knew she would need money to continue to carry out the vision God gave her, but she also knew that He would provide the tools and finances necessary to succeed. Even though she firmly believed that God was supplying her need, Mary did not sit idly by and wait for her windfall. She and her students baked sweet potato pies to sell at nearby work sites. They tended a garden and raised chickens. Some of the vegetables and eggs were sold, and the rest was used at the school for meals.

*Faith is the first factor in a life devoted to service. Without it, nothing is possible. With it, nothing is impossible*
**Mary McLeod Bethune**

Now that Mary had the land she would need, it was time to get to work. She organized a group of parents and neighbors to assist her in clearing the lot. There was much fund raising that also needed to happen. Aside from baking, Mary organized the children into a choir. She taught hymns, praise songs, and Negro spirituals that she sang in church. Little Albert sold magnolia blossoms to the crowds that gathered to listen to the students sing. He would hitch his wagon to the goat, place Spanish moss in the bed of the wagon and gather the Magnolia blossoms. The moss would keep the blossoms from bruising and he could get top price. Even at the tender age of 5, daddy had a good mind for business. It was not long before the young students attracted attention from some of Daytona's fashionable hotels. Mary also sang a few songs before speaking to the audience about their school. The young choir was even invited to the Palmetto Garden Club to entertain their guests.

God was opening many doors for Mary that confounded even those requesting her to perform. Just as the parable of the seeds, in the Bible, that fell on both good and bad ground my grandmother's speeches and requests for help were not always so well received. She did not pay these people any attention; all it meant was that her God had not chosen them to support the school. Mary shook the dust from her shoes and continued on her way.

## Daytona Normal and Industrial Institute at their barn

Now the same way that Mother Dear would have to shake the dust from her shoes about the "nay sayers", she would have to do the same as it related to my grandfather. Albertus wanted a house wife. He tried to deal with this woman of God who had visions and seemed driven in her pursuit to educate anyone that had a need. But he wanted the traditional family. It was what he was accustomed to. Now here he was making the best he could of his business and his wife, Mary Jane McLeod Bethune was putting all her energy into this dream of a school for girls... Daytona Normal Institute. It was more than he could handle. He drifted and for a while he and Mother Dear kept the pretense of a family but when Albertus decided to move back to South Carolina, Mary knew it was a trip he would make alone.

Albertus and Mary never sought divorce as that was not the custom in those days. They also worked out an agreement for Albertus to see his son during the summer months when school was not in session. Albert enjoyed time with his father as well as the extra freedoms he was given. As much fun as he had, he was still happy to return home to Daytona and his mother. Albertus lived a very quiet life until his death in 1914. My daddy was 15 years of age.

*But they that wait upon the Lord shall renew their strength; they shall mount up with wings as eagles they shall run, and not be weary; and they shall walk, and not faint Isaiah 40:31*

# I Leave You Racial Dignity

It was a busy time for Daytona Literary and Industrial School for Training Negro Girls. Mary was busy with planning upcoming lessons, baking for fundraisers and working on securing benefactors for the school. My father, Albert, had the heart and mind of a true entrepreneur. He inherited his father's keen perception and savvy for business.

God's hand guided Mary through storms and valleys. She began praying every morning while still lying under the covers. One early morning, God allowed her to see the faces – white faces – of those who would be sent to help her. Not long after, Thomas White of the White Sewing Machine Company was vacationing with his family in Daytona when they heard Mary's choirs singing in their hotel. Mr. White was impressed both by the beautiful harmonies and the intelligent and articulate African American woman who spoke passionately of a school that educated the poor and under privileged. He made an appointment to talk with Mary more in depth about her dream.

Mr. White entered her simple office as a man simply curious about her work and left as a regularly contributing benefactor of Mary's school. He asked her to "show me this school that you speak of so highly". She took him out to the vacant landfill and spoke of her vision. I later said that he saw through her eyes the hope for her people and he wanted to be a part of something great. His own company grew and flourished, I believe, because he obeyed the voice of God telling him to be a paymaster towards my grandmother's vision.   Another very well known contributor was James M. Gamble of Proctor & Gamble.  This led to others making donations to Mary as the school grew and with each passing year.  The first buildings on campus are named Faith Hall and White Hall because of what it took to make the vision real.

The school's choir was now traveling all over the state of Florida performing and raising money.  Mary was bursting at the seams with joy over seeing the manifestation of her vision.  It was no longer only for her to see, but anyone and everyone.  She now had far more than five students, a few buildings, and also staff to assist with daily business activities.   Mary was also quickly gaining notoriety in Daytona, Florida and other southern states.

Being well known was very beneficial for Mary and her school.  Sadly, it also brought unfavorable responses at a much heightened level from groups who were very displeased and did not approve of her work because of the color of her skin.  The Ku Klux Klan sent menacing and threatening correspondence to Mary, demanding she discontinue her education of "nigger" children.  The Klan did not think they needed to be taught anything, lest they forget their place.  Mary paid them no attention and refused to back down.  If God was for her, no one would be crazy enough to be against her.

In the darkness of night, as cowards roll, the Klan headed for the campus, My grandmother and the staff gathered the students together in one building and turned all the lights on so there was no doubt that they were present. They began to sing Leaning on the Everlasting Arms and This Little Light of Mine. Some of the students cried silently but sang anyway because they trusted Madame Bethune to take care of them just as she trusted God to do the same. The storm that was the Ku Klux Klan raged on before her eyes. No buildings were burned that night or any other night and the Klan did not return to Bethune-Cookman.   No one connected to the school (staff and students) was physically harmed; Mary was never accosted, not once. God kept them safe. His plan would not be stopped by anyone. Mary trusted in her faith as she always did and continued moving forward.

On June 11, 1954 my grandmother wrote to the Attorney general of the State of Florida, the following words:

*"In my judgment, the decision made by the Supreme Court of the United States regarding segregation is the greatest mandate that has been handed down since the Emancipation Proclamation. We should receive this decision with gratitude and humility. Let no spirit of arrogance be kindled within any of our hearts."* She went on to say that, *"We, (meaning the black race) are law abiding American citizens. Let us unite our minds and hearts and work out the integration of this problem in as peaceful and harmonious a manner as possible. But do not let us delay. The longer we wait, the harder the task will be to perform.   Everything necessary cannot be done at one stroke, but it must be done.  With conferences and common sense and consistency it can and will be done at last.*

*May I call to the attention of our white citizens that it is not the desire of Negroes to enter "white schools" for the purpose of association with white people. We have a dignity and a pride and a background of which we are not ashamed.*

*What we want for ourselves and for our posterity is the best sort of schools, the best possible opportunities for development into the best citizens we are capable of becoming.*

*Integration of the school groups should begin at once at the top level and then the doors should be opened right down the grades as rapidly as possible – just as soon as the necessary steps can be worked out among both Negro and white citizens in every city, town and village. No barriers should be strong enough to impede our progress."*
**Dr. Mary McLeod Bethune**

In a press release on the eve of the monumental, unanimous decision by the Supreme Court, Mary McLeod Bethune also said, *"America may hold her head higher now among the nations. From within she has been straightened. This is a matter of spiritual significance. We have officially declared ourselves ready to practice fully at home the doctrines of democracy, human dignity and equal rights which we have declared to the world as a way of life. We have abolished the hypocrisy so long eating at the heart of our own social life.*

*I rejoice as a pioneer in the field that I have lived to hear with my own ears and see with my own eyes and feel with my own heart this great, inevitable decision."*

At the time of this landmark decision I was 2 years old. I would be in junior high school when the schools of Daytona Beach began the process to fully throw the doors open for an integrated school system. In the South, court decisions meant very little and much blood would be spilled before there would be even the appearance of equal access under the law.

Moving forward for Mary McLeod Bethune would mean a full blown co-ed, 4 year college, Bethune-Cookman College, appointments to the federal government by sitting Presidents, an audience with the Pope and receipt of his blessing, national and international awards, the founding of the National Council of Negro Women and more recognition than she could have ever imagined. She never gave up, even when the odds were not in her favor. She was not banking on her ability to get the job done, she was trusting God. Her vision, her forthrightness, her leadership abilities, her ability to persevere, her insurmountable faith, were they a unique gift from God or was it on her DNA? Who would have known that the little black girl from outside of Maysville, SC would advise 4 United States Presidents, get a postage stamp with her image and a national monument in Washington, DC? Who would have known? God knew it all the time.

As my grandmother grew in stature nationally and internationally, she handpicked her successors. It was important to her that her work with Bethune-Cookman, continued to grow. She never lost sight of the fact that the "keys to freedom" lie in education. Her work with Ida B. Wells was critical in women's movements in the north and south because it organized women's groups in ways unheard of in this country. Even as she organized women's organizations in The National Council of Negro Women, it was still about education and understanding the power of being organized to move platforms forward politically and economically. Mary McLeod Bethune knew something that many of our current leaders seem to have forgotten. We are not going to live forever and if we want the institutions that we leave behind to grow and prosper and even more importantly, to continue after we are long gone, we must develop the leadership that comes behind us. We must train them to take our place and allow them to find their wings, before we die, not *because* we died.

Today, within the Black community, we are lacking strategic leadership across the board, in most of our historical institutions, not because there is a void of capable and willing young people but because we have not trained them properly to SERVE the community first. They do not have a sense of the importance of service simply because it is the right thing to do. If my grandmother had waited for acknowledgment before giving unselfishly to our people, her greatest moments may never have been realized because she would not have given God the opportunity to show off. He took the least of us and made her the best of us. For many years we listened to our parents talk about Mother Dear's accomplishments without fully understanding the magnitude and even today as we look at what God placed within her, we are still amazed and eternally grateful.

Mary McLeod Bethune

# Mary McLeod Bethune
1875 - 1955

"I leave you faith. Faith is the first factor in a life devoted to service. Without faith, nothing is possible. With it, nothing is impossible."

Excerpt from the Last Will and Testament

Not for myself                But for othe

Albert Bethune, Sr. front row, Albert Bethune, Jr. second row on the occasion of the Dedication of the Statue of Dr. Bethune in Lincoln Park, Washington, DC.

I Leave You the

Desire to

Live

Harmoniously

With Your

Fellow Man

Honored By Negro Women: Feted at the National Council of Negro Women's annual Brotherhood Luncheon in Washington, Dr. Mary McLeod Bethune, Mrs. Eleanor Roosevelt and TV star Ed Sullivan offer each other handshakes of congratulations while council president Mrs. Vivian Mason watches approvingly.

**30,000 Elks In Atlanta Honor Dr. Bethune**

Dr. Mary Bethune, 76-year-old founder of Florida's Bethune-Cookman College, became the second Negro to receive the Lovejoy award for "outstanding contributions to race relations" at the Elks national convention in Atlanta. More than 30,000 "Elks" from every section of the U.S. and many foreign countries attended the five-day meeting which highlighted: 1) the re-election of William C. Hueston, Washington, as grand secretary; 2) outlining by Grand Exalted Ruler Robert H. Johnson of plans for expansion of health, education and civil rights programs; and 3) establishing of a program to take care of "brown babies" in Germany.

*Robert Johnson and Dr. Bethune.*

Mrs. Bethune Named Top Mother: Cited as "mother of the century" by the Dorie Miller Foundation, Dr. Mary McLeod Bethune receives foundation award for achievement in Negro affairs from Dr. L. H. Bishop, last year's recipient, at Chicago's Tabernacle Baptist Church. Witnessing ceremony is Rev. E. Jerry Walker.

**Dr. Bethune Reveals Retirement Plans At Detroit**

Dr. Mary McLeod Bethune, 71-year-old, internationally-acclaimed humanitarian, revealed her retirement plans at the Alpha Chi Pi Omega beauticians' convention at Detroit. After 50 years of public life, Dr. Bethune said she is retiring to: 1) establish a Mary McLeod Bethune Foundation at Daytona Beach, Fla., to provide scholarships for students and an endowment for Bethune-Cookman College; 2) write an autobiography telling of her life's work; and 3) convert her Daytona Beach home into a shrine which will house all information about her life. Mrs. Marjorie Joyner, national supervisor of the United Beauty School Owners and Teachers Association, presented $3,830, the first donation, in behalf of the beauticians to the Bethune Foundation.

*Dr. Bethune and Mrs. Joyner*

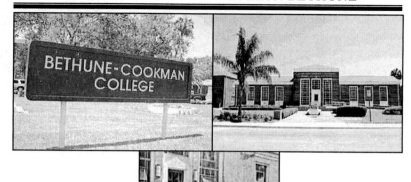

The Great Bethune Cookman University
Enter to Learn—Depart to Serve
www.cookman.edu

## 1,000 AT RITES FOR DR. BETHUNE

Some 1,000 notables and scholars flocked today into Deland, Fla., to pay final homage to Dr. Mary McLeod Bethune, dauthered-daves. Among them: Dr. Howard Thurman of Boston U., Frank S. Horne of the FHA; John Sengstacke of the Chicago Defender. With city flags at half-mast for the first time in honor of a private citizen, Dr. Bethune was buried in a grassy mound above Bethune-Cookman, the college she founded 51 years ago with only $1.50.

Albert Bethune (r) bows military honors with also son after lil the FHA; John Sengstacke of the Chicago Defender. With city flags at half-mast for the first time in honor of a private citizen, Dr. Bethune was buried in a grassy mound above Bethune-Cookman, the college she founded 51 years ago with only $1.50.

Bethune-Cookman officials carry Dr. Bethune's body from chapel. She was "greater than Booker T. Washington."

## Ex-Student Donates Casket For Dr. Bethune

A former student at Bethune-Cookman College, now a Deland, Fla., mortician, donated the full-couch bronze casket in which Dr. Mary McLeod Bethune, the school's founder, was buried. The mortician, Charles Bailey, said he gave the casket in appreciation for help he received from Dr. Bethune while he was a student at the Daytona Beach school.

## Albert Bethune, Sr. and the Elks Organization

Albert Bethune, Sr. and the
Post Master General on the day of issue for the Mary
McLeod Bethune Postage Stamp

# Finally...
# I Leave You A
# Responsibility to
# Our Young
# People

# Daytona, Bonner Elementary
# and the Bethunes

Our house and my oldest brother's house were next door to each other and there was a Bar-B-Q stand in the front yard that was run by Mr. Pinkston and his family when we were kids. Our yard was big enough to play tag football and we had plenty of space for hide and seek. Across the street was Allen Chapel AME Church and Mr. Glover's Photo Shop. On the same side of the street as the photo shop was Gainous Funeral Home and on the second floor of that building was Dr. Brunson's Dental Office and the apartment where Cousin Lucille lived. Cousin Lucille was Mother Dear's niece. We could look out of our back door at the college campus. The road that separated our house form the college was tagged the Gym Road because Moore's Gymnasium was located on the other side. There were lots of open land and plenty of perfect for skating sidewalks. When school was closed for Christmas, the campus of Bethune-Cookman served as the neighborhood gathering place because the sidewalks and open fields were the best in the neighborhood for non-stop skating, bike riding and just hanging out with your friends.

On the 4th of July we could sit on our fence and watch the fireworks that were soaring in the air from the beach. I used to wonder why we never went to the beach in Daytona to watch until I got older and realized that Black people in Daytona were not allowed on the beach after 5 p.m. unless they were working. We could not get in the ocean in Daytona. That was a WOW (**W**ith-**O**ut **W**ords) moment for me.

This was the place I knew best, the place where my heart was. "Zoom, Zoom". That was me on my bike, riding like the wind with my hair flying, headed to visit my girlfriends. We all lived within walking distance of each other and in the 1950 and 60s, all the black people we knew lived on the same side of the tracks and even though there was "south street" and "over by the college', we were still one community. Most of the children in our neighborhood went to the same nursery, Sara Hunts Nursery School, the same elementary school, Bonner Elementary, and went to the same high school, Campbell Jr. and Sr., High. If we were lucky we got to leave Daytona to go to college but if not we could go to the Mighty Bethune Cookman College or the Volusia County Vocational School.

Attending Sara Hunt's Nursery School meant that you got the best start you possibly could for an education. Behind the building that housed the nursery and pre-k classes, was the Sara Hunt Orphanage. This was the place where the children who had no one were taken care of. Because my mom was a beautician, we spent some Saturdays at the orphanage while our mother and members of the Beauty Culture Organization did the hair of the little girls at the orphanage. As children, we *adopted* these children who became our personal projects and we made sure that we remembered birthdays and special holidays with gifts and outings. Our mother was one of the most dynamic women that you would ever meet. First, she was drop dead gorgeous, even for our mother and we were glad she belonged to us. Second, she was incredibly smart and creative. She was also filled with a desire to make the world a better place and she gave that sensibility to her children.

There was another side to our mother however. There was that side of her that said to us "wherever you embarrass me, that is where I am going to embarrass you". We did not test this very often because we knew that she meant it. I have often said that in our household, mommy was the crucifixion and daddy was grace and mercy. Our mother was also one of the best cosmetologists in the city of Daytona Beach. She attended trade school in Jacksonville, FL to learn the art of beauty culture and had a broad understanding about hair and what was required not only to give you a great hair style but to keep hair on your head. She could weave magic, literally. Some of her clients had thinning hair for various reasons but when they left my mother's salon, they had beautiful hair that lasted until their next appointment which was usually two weeks.

Mommy also was not a supporter of relaxing hair. It was her professional feeling that "very little testing was occurring on Black folk's hair and we might want to proceed with caution." History has proven her correct as many can attest to their hair falling out, breaking off, scalp burns and hair not growing back. It is rumored that autopsies have shown hair relaxer underneath the scalp. I am sure that would not promote intellect and may very well account for some of the "drama" experienced in the neighborhood these days.

Now if I never talk about anything else, I have to talk about Bonner Elementary. The school was located across from Pine Haven Projects and like everything else on our side of the tracks was in need of everything except good teachers. You see, we had the best already. For me, my classroom teachers were Mrs. Armstrong, Mrs. Neal, Mrs. VanPool, Mrs. Jones, Mrs. Wesley and Mrs. Gainous. There was also, Mrs. Ryan, Mrs. Young, Mrs. Adams and so many, many more, talented and dedicated teachers whose first thought was our welfare and education. For art there was Mr. Johnson who let us draw a mural on the wall, Mrs. Wright was our Librarian, Mr. Morris taught music and made sure we knew the difference between a cello, a violin, a viola and an upright bass. We knew because he brought them to school and taught us how to play them. I even got to take a violin home so I could practice for our class recital. We also had our own resident genius in the form of Dr. Hodge who spoke several languages and could have been anywhere in the world but he was there for us, teaching us Spanish. I remember the first time I saw him teaching conversational Spanish on TV. I wondered how he got inside the box.

Mrs. LaRosa Smith was our principal and she always

had a smile for us. Even after leaving a certain grade, the next year you always went back to visit your other teachers because you loved them so much. Mrs. Rose Marie Bryant taught us Bible verses and how to be human beings instead of heathens and it worked for most of us. I would say that most of the poetry that I have committed to heart was people who could hate little children just because they happened to be black.

My first year at Bonner, 1958, just getting to first grade, I was elected Little Miss Bonner Elementary. This was the year they changed the name of the elementary school from Cypress Street Elementary in honor of Mrs. Evelyn Bonner. I really think I got elected because my niece Patricia got all her friends to vote for me. I loved school, especially Bonner. My daddy was retired so he had lots of time to spend with his children. He became the class dad and always made sure that we had what we needed. I remember in my second grade class, he had curtains made for our cloak closet and bought an aquarium with fish for our room. My teacher, Mrs. Neal was so encouraging, as were all of our teachers. They taught with a lot less than the teachers at white schools but they gave so much to us that we did not know we were working with less. By the time I was preparing for third grade I was reciting The Creation by James Weldon Johnson and I did it so well that the principal, Mrs. LaRosa Smith took me to other schools to show off my skills.

There were always opportunities for the children to

stand up in front of people and recite what we had learned. Most importantly there was an environment that nurtured us and teachers who made us feel like we could achieve anything that we set our minds to. Even the cafeteria workers took great care of us. Mrs. Newkirk made sure that no child went hungry and Mrs. Anderson could fix fish and spinach so good that you wanted to eat your vegetables. Right today, I love spinach cooked with boiled eggs in it because that was how I learned to eat it at Bonner Elementary. It was in the 6th grade, in Mrs. Gainous' class that I learned of the assassination of John F. Kennedy. I remember Mrs. Gainous being called out of our class and coming back in tears. We were afraid. When she told us that the President of the United States had been assassinated, we were in shock and we all began to cry. It was her reassurances that helped us work through what we were feeling. We were old enough and smart enough to know that this was not a good thing. It was at Bonner Elementary that we learned how to walk up and down stairs and how to enter a room. We also learned to get underneath our desks in case of an invasion or the dropping of bombs. We had evacuation drills to get us ready because during this time was the Bay of Pigs and Batista being kicked out of Cuba. He sought political asylum and moved to Miami so we had to be ready just in case that little island, 90 miles off the coast of Miami decided to attack us.

Something much worse, than the Cuban Missile Crisis, occurred during this same period. It was called "freedom of choice" and really caused a rift in the world of many black children. Wikipedia states, *"Freedom of Choice" (free transfer also)* was the name for a number of plans developed in the US during 1965-70, aimed at the integration of schools in states that had a segregated educational system." Instead of just letting us go to the traditional junior high school, some of our parents got together and decided that because of the opportunity provided by freedom of choice, now was the time to integrate/desegregate the schools in Daytona Beach. Our parents with the guidance of some school administrators decided that they would send the top students from the black elementary and junior high schools to ensure that we were able to handle the work. We were placed in white junior high and high schools in the hope that there could be a quiet change instead of forced compliance. While the school work was easy, it was the acts of physical assault such as being spit on in the hallway on your way to class, or being pushed down a flight of stairs or shoved into a locker that we were not prepared for. We were not prepared for the open hostility of most of the teachers, administrators, parents and of course our fellow students. Other than the janitor, there were no black people but us on campus. The principal, Mr. Walters was as bad as the rest. The only salvation for us was Mr. McHughes who was the most compassionate white person I had every met up to that point. He made it a point to stand in the halls when we changed classes and he always spoke kindly to us because he knew that we were afraid. Mrs. Sylvia Steele was one of the reasons that we were afraid. There was nothing that a black child could do or say in defense of their actions that she was not able to twist into a suspension for the black child. It didn't matter that you may have been defending yourself. Mr. McHughes however overturned many of her decisions. Mrs. White was my English teacher and always gave us the opportunity to speak. She never ignored a hand up, and she tried to always show us respect.

I was always grateful that every day, when I came out of that building, my daddy was there to pick me up. I did not have to walk home like many of my classmates and I did not have to be afraid that someone would pick a fight once they left the school grounds. Anger was a big part of our lives back then because we had no voice and we felt the hot sting of racism without being equipped to deal with it.

Many times we wondered out loud why our parents would send us to such an awful place. As children we could not understand why they thought we would get a better education in a place where we were not wanted and being taught by teachers who, for the most part, did not want to teach us. Many of my fellow black classmates carried the scars, mental and physical, of our time at Mainland Junior High and "freedom of choice". We were still able to shine because we did not give up or give in. We felt that we were doing something for the community, not just for ourselves. For the record, everyone was not filled with hate but many were silent in the face of it. There were many students who did not participate in the pushing and fighting or the spitting. But they also never spoke out against it. There were also teachers who gave us opportunities to participate without that feeling of hostility that we felt in some classes.

I acquired a true appreciation for the Beatles and other rock and roll groups because we exercised in our Physical Education classes to music that I normally would not have been exposed to. It is interesting that in 2008 many of the issues we faced in 1965 are still relevant as we see the re-segregation of many public schools across the country and racism still deeply embedded in the very fabric of the country.

As the grandchildren of Mary McLeod Bethune, everyone knew us. Everywhere we went, the influence of Bethune-Cookman was present. People that we encountered always referred to us as the grandchildren of Mary McLeod Bethune. We were seldom called by our names when introduced and frequently spoken about as if we were not present. Assumptions were made about our future plans with little or no input from us. For instance, on many occasions I was told, "Oh, I am sure that you want to be a teacher, just like your grandmother". The fact was that I wanted to be Diana Ross. From the time I was in elementary school, my singing buddies, Gwen Hill, Barbara Moore, LaRosa Brown, and Margaret Davis and I sang. We had a girls group and we sang the songs of the 60's. The Supremes, the Marveletts, and Martha and the Vandelas were who we modeled ourselves after. We had costumes and scenery and we knew all the lyrics. Many times we entered talent contests and on occasion were featured and not allowed to compete because we were really good.

When we got to junior high, it was the singing that helped us find our groove. We all were in the school choir and Ms. Boren was our music teacher. She let us sing and it was the music that helped us get through the hate. It also opened channels for communication that did not exist previously. Some white students started to see that the black students were not that different after all. By the time we got to senior high, some of us who started out on hostile ground actually ended up friends, like me and Mike Bledsoe. Music is universal and in many cases it does "calm the savage beast".

During the days of Jim Crow and segregation, Daytona Beach was as segregated as any other southern town and in the neighboring town of Port Orange, The Ku Klux Klan was very active and well documented. None of this meant anything to an elementary school child and especially one with a college campus as a playground. I never felt safer and spent a great deal of my time playing in the street, climbing neighborhood trees catching tadpoles in the ditch on campus. When it rained really hard, we had a swimming hole that miraculously appeared in front of the Moore's Gym because of the unleveled ground. Many of the neighborhood kids found their way past that grassy watering hole on hot days after the rain and somehow just seemed to fall in. I cannot tell you how many times our parents would say, "stay out of that dirty water before you catch something you can't get rid of". Did we care, obviously not because the best swim for a short kid who really can't swim yet is in water that is shallow enough to only cover your shin bones but if approached right can wet up all your clothes. Those were the days of summer on the campus of BCC.

As the safe haven of elementary school and the trauma of junior high moved into the hormonal changes of senior high school, the struggle between the races became less visible but it never completely subsided. The natural progression was for those students who attended Mainland Junior High to move on the Mainland Senior High School. The Mainland Senior High School Buccaneers were one of the top rated schools in Volusia County and the intent was to keep it that way. The system for attendance was still based on "freedom of choice" and most of the black students 'chose' to attend Campbell Senior High. The ones who didn't were almost seen as traitors and on many occasions fights between black students from Mainland and Campbell would break out as the school bus dropped them off in the neighborhood.

Like most plans for the integrating of schools, it would be the black community that would lose the most and have the greatest adjustment. By the time I was in the 10th grade, Campbell Street High School was closing and the students were forced into Mainland. That was the year that we had two homecoming kings and two home coming queens: one white and one black.

This was also the year that Martin Luther King, Jr. was assassinated. When the word spread through school that Dr. King had been shot, you could feel the energy become red hot. Black students walked out of class as though on cue from some unknown source. We were all looking for some solace that just did not exist. We gathered in the middle of the campus in an area set aside for seniors only. On any other day, under classmen caught in the seniors only area could be totally embarrassed by upper classmen, but not this day. Even those who may have had the thought quickly let it go as they looked into the faces of the black students gathered in that space. Teachers and counselors were present but many were feeling exactly what the students were feeling and had no words to make it better. In that moment, for many of the students gathered in that space and black people all over the country, hope for a better world, a world where the color of person's skin did not matter more than the content of ones character, disappeared. Dr. King was the peace maker. He was the one who tried to bring us all together. If they (the white man) would kill the peace maker, maybe it was not peace that they wanted after all.

All over the country, there were eruptions of violence, even in Florida. Most of us did not think we would ever see normal again, whatever normal was. But life goes on. By the time I got to the 12th grade I had been in and out of love a couple of times, the love of my life being an upper classman named Curtis. When in 11th grade I came around a corner going to my next class and Curtis was hugging one of my best friends, Wanda, I felt like I had swallowed a hot coal. That feeling stayed with me for a very long time. I don't think I every stopped loving Curtis, even when he stopped loving himself and was taken over by drugs and mental illness. I have never known what happened to him but will always give thanks for the effort he made, even in the midst of his own trauma, to make sure our daughter was taken care of. The battle that he waged with the Social Security office to get her added to his SSI benefits speaks to the depths of his love for his child and even though he had become known for acts of violence and temper, he never tried to harm me or his daughter. His counselors said that some of his calmest moments were when he had interacted with us. We like to believe that it was because he knew we really cared and even to this day pray that his spirit has found the peace it deserves.

Although I was academically smart, I have never been really street smart and by the time I reached 12th grade, I was looking forward to escaping Daytona Beach. I spent a great deal of time on the campus of Bethune Cookman. I was very attractive and though only 5'3, I had legs to die for. I was also very much attracted to older men and they were attracted to me. In my house the only dialog about sex was not to do it. Well like the term, "just say no' it is a lot easier to say it than do it. My mother grew up in the era when nobody talked about sex and all you knew was that it was taboo. That of course did not mean that you didn't do it. You just did not let any body know that you were doing it. It was pretty much that way in the neighborhood as a whole. Girls were told to keep their skirts down and their panties up. The reward for doing this was a blessing from God and the Debutants' Ball.

I was very monogamous in my relationships because I always thought I was in love and that I was being loved in return. I know now of course that I was probably in lust and did not know the difference until it was way into the relationship. I was fortunate enough (some would not agree with the word fortunate in this case) to have lost my virginity to a man who was more concerned with my satisfaction than his own and so my first experience was a great experience. The down side is that once the horse is out of the corral it is hard to get it back in and it's the same with great sex. Once you know what that is, it is hard not to want it again. My mother did her absolute best to keep me in the corral. She begged, whipped, put me on punishment and just plain cussed me out. Many times when she thought I was out doing something she didn't like, I was just avoiding coming home to hear her fuss. There were times when I was just sitting on the beach watching the waves and feeling the peace. To this day, I hate confrontation and still avoid it if possible. I have learned however that some confrontation is good for the soul. My mother was fighting a losing battle. She forgot what ends she had gone to when she was my age, to be with the one she loved. You see, sex is not the bad thing that people make it out to be in fact it can be quite good. The bad part is having sex when you are not ready and ill prepared for the consequences. As a teenager, physically developed but mentally unprepared, I graduated from high school, 8 months pregnant. I was pregnant for a man, fully grown, in college, handsome as Shaka Zulu and totally unprepared to deal with a pregnant teenager. Tony graduated from BCC in 1970 with the full knowledge of my pregnancy as we talked about it for months before he left and went back to south Florida. He has only seen his beautiful daughter once and she was just a baby sleeping in her crib. But fate is a really funny thing.

When Liz was attending BCC, she met her brother Kevin and they communicate to this day. I am sure that there were many things that kept Tony from acknowledging his daughter, the prime reason being that he had a family and he was considered an adult while I was not out of high school yet. To be clear, he never took advantage of me and was always careful and used protection but sometimes, as they say, stuff happens. I am grateful because I would not take anything for the beauty that is found in my children but the one thing I know for sure, babies having babies is not a good way to bring children into the world. I was not prepared to raise children on my own.

I say this to my sisters who may read this book.

It is the woman who carries that child for 9 months and generally it is the woman who never walks away. There are exceptions but they are few and far between. If a brother decides that he does not want to do the right thing, he can just get up and go. I never tried to force the fathers of my girls to pay child support because I always felt like I could do it by myself. I was wrong. Curtis did the best he could to care for his child. Tony, on the other hand, never looked back. My behavior came out of a feeling of being displaced. I was looking for where I belonged. Being needy makes it easy to be courted, because it's the words more than the actions on which you are focused. I was a sexy little teenager, living across the street from a college campus. It was too much temptation. My actions and the trouble I got into were not because my parents were bad parents or because they did not do their job. It was because we were all in the same boat. My dad had to look at all the work of his mother, remember the effort that he had put into the growth and development of the Great Bethune Cookman College, and in the latter part of his life worry about how he was going to provide for his family. Do you think that was his mother's intent when she was preparing for the future of the college and her family? As for my mother, she had dreams of her own that she deferred because she fell in love with my daddy and had a house full of children that she would have given her last breath to ensure their safety and that they were provided for in the best manner. She often talked about how she wanted to have a bigger salon that could provide all the services to black women that the white salons provided but there was never enough money to go beyond her one station.

Our mother always looked like a million dollars and she made sure that daddy was always looking good. When money was very tight and they could not afford to get everybody new coats or new clothes, our parents always put the children first. One winter, my mother did not have a coat because she wanted to make sure that we had warm clothing first. Their sacrifices to ensure that we never felt left out or that we even knew how poor we were are chiseled in our souls and will never be forgotten.

As the grandchildren of Mary McLeod Bethune, one of the greatest women who ever lived, we were always struggling. I watched my parents as they tried to provide not only for us but for my Brother Albert, Jr.'s children also. One of my nephews still feels the sting of being excluded. He remembers never being taken to a ball game by my brother. Never doing the father and son things that families do. Very early in his life he got a job so he could have nice clothes like the young boys he went to school with, and as soon as he was old enough, he left and did not come back for a very long time. We were Bethunes and people expected us to participate in community at a certain level but many times we couldn't. Not because we didn't want to but because we could not afford to do so. Sometimes we would not talk about events because we knew we could not afford it. When mommy would find out, she would sign us up and then go into over drive to make it happen. My mother was magic. She worked miracles. She used lay-a-way plans like people use credit cards. She was always planning ahead and making sure we had the best. We did not know what K-Mart was until we started shopping for ourselves. Mommy always said that if you buy the best, it lasts longer and looks better as it ages.

Events like Fashionetta and Jabberwock were annual social fundraisers, sponsored by the Alpha Kappa Alpha and Delta Sigma Theta Sororities. These were two of the prime events every year and all the little girls wanted to be a part of the center stage. My mother made sure that I participated, even though winning the title of Little Miss Fashionetta or Little Miss Jabberwock meant that she had to organize her community committee women and sell dinners, pies, and candy apples to raise money. She also was the best ticket seller on the planet. It also meant that she was going to be present when the money was counted because it was not unusual for someone who wanted their daughter to win, to write a check on the spot, after the deadline, to push their child over the top. I am not sure if mommy knew how much her children trusted her to make everything right in the world, but we did and she never let us down.

On the other hand, we felt that we let her down on many occasions. Our mother wanted the best for us and when she found out that I was pregnant, her fear was that, like her, I would not graduate from high school. In 1970 it was not acceptable for girls to attend day school when they were expecting. You had to attend night school and you could not participate in graduation. It was only God's grace and the silence of my teachers that made it possible for me to stay with my class to finish. They never said a word and when I needed encouragement there was always someone there to say, hang in there. I marched across the stage in June 1970, with honors and gave birth to my first daughter in July 1970. *"I know der is a God"*

My mother was more hurt than angry and when it was time for me to go to the hospital she would not come with me, but my daddy was right there. The first face I saw when I came out of the delivery room was daddy, sitting in a chair with his cane in hand and that wonderful smile of love on his face. I don't know what my daddy was like before I was born. Some people say that he was arrogant and spoiled by his mother. I can't speak to that because from the day I was born until the last breath that he took, he never stopped showing us how much he loved us. There was nothing that we could not tell him. Even when he did not like what we had to say, he listened. Mommy used to say that there was nothing he loved more than his children and that if he only had $5 and bought ice cream, he was going to bring it back home to his family. People came to our house all the time to ask for his help especially, if their children got in trouble with the law or if they needed help to understand legal documents. They trusted that "Bert Bethune" would make a phone call or point them in the right direction. He always did.

I don't ever remember my daddy speaking harshly about anyone, not even the people who treated him with disrespect. His greatest hurt was the day he went to his mother's house and the locks had been changed and no one had bothered to tell him. Mrs. Bronson was the curator during the tenure of her husband, Oswald Bronson, as President and she had asked daddy if he would be there to greet visitors because no one living knew more about his mother than him. Every week day, daddy went to the Foundation and would talk with students and visitors about Mary McLeod Bethune. Daddy was in his seventies but he was still driving himself around and loved being on campus. The day that he was locked out of the house that he had spent his life going in and out of; this was the day I started to hate Bethune Cookman Administration. It was the day that I saw my daddy's heart break because of selfishness. Over the years, I watched people profess to be Christians and yet behave like the Pharisees. This was one of those moments. Daddy was told that he would receive a new key but never did. No one ever had the common decency to ever explain why. It was just another act of disrespect to the Bethune family.

Right after Mother Dear died and before the twins were born, I remember all of the family having to go to the courthouse for a hearing concerning Mother Dear's Will. It was all the great-grands, Betty and Albert, Jr., and me, mommy and daddy. This was for the reading of the will. It was also when the court appointed the attorneys to manage the Trust Fund which was established for the grands and great-grands. This trust fund was to be distributed when the youngest great grand turned twenty one. By the time the attorneys finished with the trust fund, there was little left to distribute. Here we were, these little black children with court appointed white lawyers, in 1955. I wonder how much they really cared about whether or not we received anything from the work of our grandmother. When that trust fund was divided between us, each of us received about $2500. Not much coming from a trust that contained stocks and bonds and real estate as well as investments in insurance companies and community news papers. There has never been a reconciliation given to the recipients of those trust fund proceeds and because we were so young and inexperienced, we did not know to ask for one. Many people have gotten rich from the work of hands but none of them were related to her and none of them reached out to her family in the manner that Mary McLeod Bethune reached out to them. There are many lessons that have been learned over the course of my life and I am sure that there are many more before I die, but the one that I have learned for sure is the importance of treating people the way that I want to be treated, whether they deserve it or not for it is not for me to judge. My grandmother gave many chances to those who deserved it and to those who did not, but she let God decide who was on what side of the line.

As children and teenagers, we hung out with the children of many of the community leaders such as the first Black attorney in Daytona, Horace E. Hill, the owner of the first black print shop, the Wesley's, The children of the President of Bethune Cookman, The Moore's, and the children of other professionals in the black community. We did not really think about status until we reached junior high and then it was more about belonging and having the cool clothes than who somebody's moms and dads were. It was primarily when we were at the home of the Moore's that we felt inadequate. We got to see the lush life style close up and the truck coming from the college with cases of food and juice and other things that were truly luxury items for us. It was also when we were denied access to places that we had always gone that we became aware of status and that as the founders grandchildren, we really did not have any say on the campus of the college she founded.

My brothers remember being kicked out of the gym by security guards; it was the same gym that they frequented since they were big enough to hold a basketball. Many times the comment was made "don't expect to be treated special just because you are Dr. Bethune's relatives." Although we never expected to be treated special, we certainly expected that our dad, Dr. Bethune's only child, would be treated special. We expected that when visitors came on campus and asked if there were any living relatives of Mary McLeod Bethune that they would not be told that no one knew how to get in touch with them since my brother worked on campus and our house where my dad lived was within spitting distance. This is an attitude that comes from the top down and is anchored in fear that there will be less light shining on them if any shines on the Bethunes. If my tone seems a bit angry I am sure that I am, though I find great release in finally writing what I and my siblings have felt for so many years.

Many of the friends of Dr. Moore and even his children attended BCC without taking out student loans. That was not true for her grandchildren and great grandchildren during the tenure of Dr. Richard V. Moore. The Bethune children have always been good and sometimes great students so grades would not ever have been an issue. When Dr. Oswald Bronson took over the reins as President it was less of a struggle and it was under his administration that I attended Bethune Cookman and earned my degree. I too have student loans from attending Bethune Cookman and so do my daughters and my nieces and nephews. It has only been with Dr. Reed at the helm that the Bethune family has begun to feel a spirit of inclusion because she has made it evident that it is acceptable to welcome Bethunes to the circle.

I am sure that there is still work to be done as there are still people on campus who have the old attitude and are not afraid to express it. My grand niece was told that she would not be hired for a job she applied for on campus because she was a Bethune. The

HR Director hired her anyway because she was qualified but she was treated so harshly by that administrator that she quit. That has been the battle of the Bethune children for as long as I can remember. We have never asked anyone to make an exception for us but to simply give us a chance.

Throughout my personal struggles, education was an important factor in my life. With two toddlers, I still knew I had to get an education in order to provide a better life for them. I applied to Bethune-Cookman in 1970, but never got an answer so I enrolled in Daytona Beach Community College in 1971. I did well and was encouraged by Dr. Ted Schiess and many others to press on. On many occasions however, the struggle seemed too much but I never gave up. In 1974 I moved to Atlanta, GA because my best girlfriend at that time, Deborah Edwards called one day and said that it was the place to be for black people. Work was easy to find and pay was good. At the time, I was on welfare, struggling to go to school and care for my little babies. The Christmas of 1973 I was given a Christmas tree for my girls but we were so broke that I could not afford decorations. I bought a roll of aluminum foil and made ornaments by rolling the foil into different size balls and hung them from the tree. My Landlord brought us a food basket and the blessing of toddlers is that they like anything shiny so they loved the tree. But my heart was breaking because I knew I could do better and had to do better for them.

In January I asked my mother if she would care for my oldest child. My youngest, I left in the care of my wonderful sister, Theodora. My plan was to go to Atlanta, get a great job and bring my babies to live with me. No one told me that Atlanta was much colder than Daytona, and it was hard to find work in the middle of the winter in a place that you knew nothing about. This was my first time leaving Daytona and moving away from all that was familiar to me. But I was determined, and God was always looking out.

I moved in with Deborah and started working through Temp Agencies. Then I got a really great job with Wyeth Drug Company. I learned to catch the bus and began the journey into independence. There were many life challenges as is normally when the child begins to become an adult and Atlanta had many more pit falls than the little town of Daytona. The beauty however was that the ATL also had incredible people, many of whom became my friends. I saw, for the first time in my life, huge numbers of black people in downtown Atlanta, dressed in suits, carrying brief cases and doing the things that I had only seen white people doing in Daytona. They were running things and making the decisions without having to look at the white person before saying anything. That was major for me. Even though I grew up in a house of entrepreneurs and saw all kinds of people in and out of our house, when I went into the businesses of Daytona, there were seldom any black people in charge or making any decisions. In fact when I was a teenager, I can't remember seeing a black clerk in any department store in Daytona. Atlanta was so different. I remember calling my mother long distance, from the Sears Store in the West End Mall just to tell her that the pictures of the manager and assistant managers were all black. I had never seen anything like that before. For a black person coming from the small segregated towns of the south, Atlanta was like going to Mecca. It was truly all that and a bag of chips. It is still that way for me even today. But as much as I loved Atlanta, I also missed my girls and the cost of living was a lot more than in Daytona. My daddy also reminded me constantly that no matter how good a job I had, I would only advance so far without a college degree.

By this time I was head over heels in love with Lee Howard, Jr., a man who was the most magnificent bass player, next to Larry Graham, that I had ever seen. He also loved me enough to agree to move back to Daytona Beach so that I could be with my daughters. That was 1976. We returned to Daytona just as the new President of Bethune-Cookman was taking his position and the opportunity to finally enroll in the college founded by my grandmother presented itself. I became officially a Wildcat in May 1976. Lee stayed in Daytona for a year, trying to find gigs but there was nothing there for him compared to the opportunities of Atlanta and the studio work that was available. Finally in 1977, he moved back to Atlanta and life for me and my rapidly growing daughters fell into the routine of school for us all, homework, laundry and an occasional date. I loved school and I excelled. I graduated Suma Cum Laude in

April of 1979.

My matriculation was fun and it was filled with moments to just really enjoy being a college student even though I was older than many of my class mates. I chose to major in accounting because I still did not want to be a teacher. I also had to deal with the humiliation of sitting in the finance office every semester to negotiate my ability to attend school, get my books and get all of my financial aid documents processed. Every semester it was the same and I was always required to get a student loan. I also was a work study student working for the accountants that were auditing the college. Anderson Hill was my supervisor and he later became the in-house attorney for the college after they arranged for him to attend the University of Florida. He was one of the first African Americans to graduate from U of F with an MBA and a Jurist Doctorate. He later became the scapegoat for a financial fiasco which sent him to federal prison and became the makings of his own book, entitled *"In Search of the Truth: A Real Life Story About What an Attorney Should Not Do!"* In May of 1979 I began work with IBM Corporation in Boca Raton, FL. I might also add that I got married to Julius Sessoms III (whom I often refer to as Julius #1) in March of the same year and we stuck it out for almost 3 years until I decided that the verbal and physical abuse would only end when I left him, so I did. Though he never hit me, his physical presence and harsh manner in talking to me, always made me feel that he might. In his later years he has become the wonderful person that I always knew he could be and for that I give thanks.

As the story goes, "my life ain't been no crystal stair" but there has been far more good than bad, and the lessons learned have helped me to find my inner strength. My head-strongness has cost me much more than it was worth to just be right or have my way and I have learned what my parents, grandparents and great grand parents knew, God must be at the center of all that you do and there are no short cuts. Each relationship must be handled above board and with honesty or the success will be short lived and the consequences eternal. I spent most of my life trying to be whatever I thought would please the people I loved. I never felt like I belonged or was connected to where I should have been. Each time I tried to be a part of the legacy left to us, I was either denied or ignored and the hurt just kept stacking up. Several of Mary's grandbabies applied for employment at the College only to be ignored, never receiving even an acknowledgement of application. We watched as the children of administrators, friends of those children and almost anyone else could find a place. Many of the members of my family completely extricated themselves from any connection with the college and other organizations related to Mary McLeod Bethune. It was too painful to try to gain acceptance.

After several short lived marriages, I also had to understand that love or lust is never enough. Both parties must bring completeness to the table and not come in looking to change the other person or to be "made whole" by the other person. God makes me whole and is the center of my joy. That knowledge allows me to smile in the midst of the storm and though I still don't always get it right, I still have work to do, on myself. I am so much better than I ever thought I could be. I also know what I want in my next life partner, and what I have to offer. I finally know that I also have value. Through all of the ups and downs in my life, my twin brothers have been there to move my furniture, help with my children and help me keep the faith. As I watched them grow, they always seemed to help me grow.

## The Twins - Two are Better than One

The twins, Hobson and Robert, were four years behind me in school so when I was in 6th grade they were in 2nd grade. Mrs. Robinson was their teacher and they loved her. Initially it was suggested to my mother that she separate them into different classes. She refused. My brothers truly enjoyed being together as they still do today. They are identical and though different in some ways, quite the same in many others. It was always interesting watching them as they went about their activities. They never had to speak to each other to know what to do. If one went right the other went left and they would meet in the middle. This ability was an excellent tactic when you're on a mission to search and destroy. "The twins" as they were often referred gave new meaning to being of one mind. They knew early on that no one, including our mother, could tell them apart so if you asked a question of one and he did not know the answer, the other one would answer for him. They carried this tactic through high school when they would switch out classes and girlfriends. But that is another book. The beauty of my brothers is that they are kind and loving, sometimes to a fault because they have often sacrificed themselves for the happiness of others. They are also gentlemen. The flip side is that they believe that they are my big brothers because there are two of them and one of me.

Hobson McLeod Bethune was named for his Godfather, Hobson Reynolds who was the Grand Exalted Ruler of the Elks in the 60's. Robert Lafayette Bethune is named for his Godfather Robert Lafayette Johnson, First Black police detective in Ohio. They were surrounded by men who were older and had great achievements. They also were blessed to be born to a father who had matured by the time we came into the world. Daddy was there for us. He was there to take us to ball games and come to school activities. Our daddy took us with him on Saturday to do laundry and he was always there to talk. As children, the twins were always on the go. Being on a college campus always provided opportunities for entertainment and Bethune Cookman was no exception. During pledge season my brothers were known to join the Delta Sigma Theta (DST) pledge line, walking behind the pledges mocking the stepping and quacking like a duck. You see, the women of DST were made stronger and bonded as sisters as they strolled the sidewalks of BCC, dressed immaculately, not a stand of hair out of place, carrying their crimson and cream ducks, doing a step, step, squat, quack routine. This was totally fascinating to the twins. The twins also enjoyed sneaking out of the house at night and going to the "Tree of Knowledge". This was a huge oak tree in front of Cookman Hall. At that time, Cookman Hall was the men's dorm and The Tree of Knowledge was a gathering place where the brothers congregated to "shoot the breeze'. One can only imagine what the twins learned under that tree. This was also the place that they learned to imitate Omega Psi Phi "Q Dogs" as they practiced their step routines. The social psychology of hanging out in the late 60s and 70s with men from varied backgrounds and being able to listen if not participate in conversations that ranged from dating to politics was, I am sure, thought provoking and in some cases character shaping. It was also one facet of community education.

One of my favorite "twin stories" is about grand theft auto. At the tender age of 14 the twins decided to borrow daddy's car. We lived in a two story garage apartment house. The family lived upstairs and rented out the apartments downstairs to college students. Right outside the window of the twins' bedroom was a tree that was excellent as an escape route, so when the twins thought that mommy and daddy were asleep, they would "borrow" the keys, climb out the window, push the car out of the yard and go for a joy ride. Now on this particular evening, it was very cold but that would not stop Hobson and Robert. You see, they had each other to support their activities and out the window they went. This time however, they did not want to be alone so they picked up a couple of their 14 year old friends and instead of just riding the neighborhood, they had the wonderful idea to visit Ormond Beach which is about 10 miles from our house. It is also the location of our mommy's best friends.

Barely seeing over the dash board, the twins and friends drive to Ormond and cruise around, having the time of their lives because they have put one over on mommy and daddy. Well, as they passed the home of one of mommy's friends, Ms. Mercedes Douglas, they are spotted. Immediately Mrs. Mert calls mommy. The conversation went like this:

**Mommy**: Hello

**Ms. Mert:** Hey Beth, is your car in the yard and are the twins at home?

**Mommy:** Of course they are. Do you know how late it is?

**Ms. Mert:** Beth you might want to check, I think I just saw them pass my house with two other boys in the car...I'll hold on.

Now at this point I cannot print the words that came out of the mouth of our mommy. But what I will tell you is that George Carlin had nothing on our mother. As she went into ninja mode, she closed the window in their room and locked it. She then made sure that all the doors and windows that they might have access to were locked. She got her favorite mode of corporal punishment ready, Daniel Green house shoes, and waited. Now this is where the telling gets to be hilarious. Thinking that they have out witted the adults, the twins push the car back in the yard; climb the tree to their room and BAM! discover that the window is locked. Immediately they know that the Ninja Mommy is awake and on the hunt. At first they decide to delay the inevitable by sleeping in the car but it is too cold so finally they come upstairs and "RING THE DOOR BELL".

The front of our house had an enclosed front porch and was just about the length of our house. As our loving mommy approached the door to open it, she was carrying, in her right hand, her Daniel Green house shoe. She let them both in but no further than the front porch. Keep in mind that they are already cold because they tried to delay as much as possible. There is nothing worse than getting "whupped" on a cold night to the tune of: "what did I tell you about stealing that car... how many times do I have to tell you, hush that crying, stop all that noise". Now add the sound of laughter because that is a sister's duty when the brothers who set your doll's hair on fire, get a whuppin'. What my mother did to them will go down in history. She *whupped* them until she got tired, rested and started again. It was what legions are made of. I am sure that the children of the 50s and 60s have many similar stories and we are all alive to talk about it and probably much better people because there was someone in our lives who could make you stop whatever you were doing, from across the room, with just one look. Our mother was a master at this. She also always would say "this hurts me more than it hurts you". No possible way!

In spite of the all the twins did to maintain their reputations of being notorious, they survived childhood and grew up to be men who care. Right out of high school, Hobson went into the Marine Corp but not before marrying Audrey. Robert was going to go to college but after about a month without Hobson, he too joined the U. S. Marines. He managed to get to Parris Island for boot camp before Hobson left. I often say that Robert joined the Marines so they could continue to dress alike, even as adults. Robert also got married to Ernestine Nunn. One of their favorite Boot Camp stories will tell you how very much they look alike.

One wonderful day, Robert is in the chow line and Hobson's commander starts chewing him out for being in the wrong line. Robert begins explaining when his Drill Instructor (DI) comes over and say to the other Drill Instructor, "why are you yelling at my recruit?" The response is "what do you mean your recruit? This is my guy and he is in the wrong place." Robert then informs them that he has an identical twin that came into the Corp; just a few weeks before him. The D.I.s made him find Hobson and bring him back to the chow hall. They stand them next to each other and say…"don't tell us we got two of you in here". Both of the twins graduated "Leather Neck" in their class. That's Marine talk for top graduate. The twins probably thought this was nothing, compared to having to follow in my path coming through high school. Robert received an honorable discharge from the Marines after 14 years in the Corp. He received a partial disability for a service related injury due to partial loss of hearing in one ear. Hobson retired as a Master Gunny Sergeant after 28 years of exemplary service to our country. The

Bethune/McLeod men have continued to serve this country in extraordinary ways from the time of enslavement up to now. Military service has included Albert Bethune, Sr., Albert Bethune, Jr., Samuel Bethune, Hobson and Robert Bethune, Rashad Bethune and Christopher Bethune in the immediate family line.

Today, Hobson and Robert are still the most wonderful brothers I could ask for and they have always stood by me or even stood for me when I could not stand for myself. Their *twinship* still makes life interesting and for sure, never dull.

*Till Death Do Us Part  -  Mr. and Mrs. Albert Bethune, Sr.*
Over 40 years of Marriage
"What's Love Got to Do With It?..... EVERYTHING!!!!"

Mr. Albert McLeod
Bethune, Sr.
Only biological child of
Mary McLeod Bethune
Born: February 3, 1899
Freed: October 31, 1989

Mrs. Elizabeth Sterricks
Bethune
Wife of Albert Bethune, Sr.
Born: December 7, 1919
Freed July 22, 1990

Those were the days but …
THE BEST IS YET TO COME!

Evelyn Bethune—1979
First Grand Child of the founder to graduate from
Bethune-Cookman College
Dr. Oswald P. Bronson  Conferring Degree

Baby Sister
Sara Bethune-Smith

Sara's Oldest Son and his family: Jarvis Smith, his beautiful wife Andrea and their newest addition Ayanna

The youngest handsome son:
Christopher Harold.

The middle son, LeNard Harold, daughter Janai and wonderful wife, Junelle.

# Bethunes some More

Elizabeth Victoria Bethune, daughter of Dr. Evelyn Bethune graduates from Bethune Cookman College  April 2005

Dr. Mary McLeod Bethune Transitional Center for Homeless Children in Long Beach, CA— *May the work I've done speak for me!*

County of Los Angeles Supervisor Don Knabe and Dr. Evelyn Bethune at the dedication of the Dr. Mary McLeod Bethune Transitional Center for Homeless Children in Long Beach, CA— Long Beach Unified School District

The Peace Academy Long Beach Unified School District

## More Bethunes

## Sara's Smile

Now baby Sister Sara had the most difficult progression to adulthood as she was the last child born to Albert Sr. and Elizabeth. When Sara was born, daddy was 62 years old and mommy was 42. Initially the doctor told mother that she was going through menopause and was not pregnant but as time progressed, mommy knew the signs of pregnancy and insisted on a pregnancy test. Due to the advanced ages of both parents there were many concerns for the health of the mother and the child but Sara made it into this world without great fanfare and in perfect health.

For me the birth of another Bethune girl was delightful. I felt that the playing field was now being equalized. My niece Pat and I could not wait for Sara to get home from the hospital so when we were allowed to ride to the hospital with daddy to visit mommy and Sara, imagine how upset we were to find out that they did not allow children into the maternity ward. The room that mommy was in had a window and Pat and I were determined to see Sara, so we went outside the one story building, found the window that was mommy's room, climbed on the hedges so we could see and looked in. Of course we got caught but the nurses realized how badly we wanted to see Sara and let us come into the room to see her for just a moment. In those days you had to stay in the hospital for at least a week and because mommy had a cesarean section, it took a bit longer. Finally the day came for them to come home and I could not wait.

Every day I would rush home from Mainland Junior High so I could help take care of Sara. Mommy had help from Aunt Esther Speed who had been helping take care of us for as long as I can remember. There were many strong women who came through our house in various categories but they all had their own flavor. Some of these wonderful women were, Miss Bertha Nixon, who not only could cook food to die for but was no joke when it came to cleaning a house, Aunty Bunch Grey, who drove us to school when daddy could not, Ms. Sadie Reese, a retired New York cab driver who was one of mommy's customers and social friends. There are so many more women who gave us a glimpse of their lives as they touched ours. Many times we stayed at Miss Bertha's house when mommy had to work or just needed a break from the antics of the Bethune clan. Aunt Esther became the Godmother for the twins when they were born and continued to help raise us throughout our lives. She was a walking testimony and never hesitated to give honor to God. It was Aunt Esther and her cousin, Mrs. Long who taught us to fish in the various tributaries in Volusia County. Mrs. Long was blind but she could bait a hook better than a sighted person. There were many fun filled days spent at the home of Aunt Esther and Mrs. Long.

We always knew when we were going to go cane pole fishing because the night before, we had to dig earth worms in the back yard. There were times when the earth worms would be as long as snakes but we never let Aunt Esther know that we were scared of them. Kenny lived next door to Aunt Esther and went to school with me. I always had a crush on him but I would have died if he ever found out. Kenny grew up to be a great man in the community and Post Master at the oldest post office in Daytona.

Aunt Esther always made sure that I could have time with Sara. Pat and I would sit on the front porch of our house for hours holding Sara, talking to her, letting her swing in her baby swing set or just reading to her. I loved her then and I love her now. Like most sisters, separated by years and sometimes location, we had our ups and downs but even when we didn't like each other, we loved each other. As Sara grew up I am sure she felt the pressure of not only the shadow of Mother Dear but also, the twins and me. She was, after all, following in our footsteps. She went to the same schools and had many of the same teachers but her talent was her won. Sara took to playing the piano like the infamous duck takes to water. It was a natural thing for her. Mother managed to always have musical instruments around us as children and it was the same when Sara came along. All through junior high and high school Sara played the piano and sang in the choir. She was delightful to be around until 10th grade.

Then something changed and Sara and I no longer connected. I am sure that part of it was the need to have her own space and be her own person but I missed her a lot. When she entered Bethune-Cookman as a music major, none of us were surprised. The struggle to get her into school was great because contrary to popular belief, there was no guaranteed place for the founder's grandchildren or great grand children. We always had to place pressure on

Mr. Ernest Cook, who was VP of the Finance Office, in order to get registered for school. He was our point of contact. There were no "special arrangements" for the founder's family and he helped where he could but it was the decision of the President as to how our accounts were handled, not his. We always felt as if we were placed in a position of begging for what should have been unquestioned… an education for the direct descendents of Dr. Mary McLeod Bethune. The hope was that we would just go away. I remember Pat saying that she would be finished paying off her student loan about the time her son, Christopher, would be ready for college.

Sara started college right after me, though she had been a part of the college gospel choir for two years before actually entering college. Her wonderful alto voice and the fact that our big brother was the founder and coordinator of the choir made that a bit easier than many of our other interactions on campus. Sara struggled at Bethune-Cookman to find her place. There were too many references to her being not just the granddaughter of the founder but also the sister of Evelyn. Many times her own personality got lost in the mix and the hostility between us only made it harder for her. She changed her major to criminal justice and not long after that dropped out of school. Like me, Sara had a hard time finding her space and knowing that she had value as a person outside of being the granddaughter of Dr. Mary McLeod Bethune. In the search for her own identity she entered into abusive relationships where the only beauty was the three magnificent sons that she bore.

My sister is one of the strongest women I know. She has a heart filled with great compassion but for a long time the hurt of relationships gone bad, stalled her personal growth. Today however, Sara has learned to take charge of her own life. She is taking computer classes and who knows, she may someday feel inclined to get her degree from BCU. But even if she never wants a college degree, what she has to give is not dependent on graduation for she has a story of her own that is filled with strength and achievement.

To give you an insight into the beauty of Sara, I must tell this story about us as a team. When my daughter, Elizabeth entered Bethune-Cookman, she had just graduated from American High in Miami. We lived in Miami for about 5 years before she graduated and she was excited about going to the school founded by her great grandmother. Well as luck would have it some of the students that she knew in Miami were also at Bethune-Cookman and they all sort of hung out together.

One day Liz was in the Mall, walking to her car and this young woman shoots at her, yelling and screaming about some young man. Fortunately, my daughter was not injured or worse, killed over something stupid. As it turned out that the young man in question and Liz had known each other in high school. They were never anything more than friends but the shooter was over the top jealous. When Liz tried previously to explain, she was met with the same type of hostility so she went on with her life. Now imagine yourself in my shoes. Your daughter comes home, hysterical talking about some crazy girl shooting at her in the parking lot of the Mall. My first question was..."Are you all right and my second question was... "Do you know where she lives?" I called Sara and told her what happened and even though I may not have been one of her favorite people at that time, this was about family. Sara came by to pick me up and we went to the shooters house. At this time Sara was a corrections officer at the county jail and was well trained in dealing with bad behavior. I on the other had, was not about to let some ignorant behavior take the life of my child because of being stuck on stupid. I am sure that the shooter was totally thrown backwards when she opened her door and Sara and I were standing there. We explained some basics to her like, jail, expulsion from school and the possibility of her own imminent physical danger and then we made her call her mother. Liz never had any other problems with her.

Sara has always been there even when she might be mad with me, we have always been sisters. I give thanks that God is always in control and at this time and place, Sara and I have found our sisterhood again and I am grateful for it.

# Today and the Future of Black America

The 2008 state of Black America was best described as resembling that of a patient on life support. The year 2009 has been even more devastating to our family structure and our Children of Promise. The most vital organ that we have is our youth and we are watching them languish and in many cases die or are killed as we debate the need to resuscitate. We have watched the jail trail out pace the race to college and marriage before having children become obsolete. The desire for an education is waning while the number of drive by shootings and drug related crimes have hit all time highs. Many say that the people have lost hope and that our young people are disconnected.

The reality is that our young people are not all failing nor or they all going to jail. Many are in college and doing extraordinary things. Across the country young adults are engaged in the issues of the day, they are writing books, blogging and developing internet communities. Yet even as the sun shines, there are dark clouds on the horizon. The HIV/AIDS rate in the United States is higher than at least 3 African nations and the group leading the way is heterosexual African Americans.

*HIV statistics tell the story of the HIV/AIDS epidemic. For African Americans in the United States, the HIV/AIDS epidemic is rapidly becoming a health crisis. AIDS data shows that in 2002, HIV/AIDS was among the top 3 causes of death for African American men aged 25 to 54 years and among the top 4 causes of death for*

African American women aged 25 to 54 years. Back then it was the number 1 cause of death for African American women aged 25 to 34 years. The HIV statistics are quite sobering. HIV/AIDS among African Americans is becoming a desperate problem. Here are some HIV facts to prove we have a lot of work to do.

## AIDS Facts and Statistics

Here are some facts about HIV among the African American Community.

African Americans accounted for 49 percent of the 42,514 estimated AIDS cases diagnosed in the United States (including US dependencies, possessions, and associated nations.
What is AIDS and What Causes It?

The rate of AIDS diagnoses for African American adults and adolescents was 10 times the rate for whites and almost 3 times the rate for Hispanics. The rate of AIDS diagnoses for African American women was 23 times the rate for white women. The rate of AIDS diagnoses for African American men was 8 times the rate for white men.
Are HIV and AIDS the Same Thing?
HIV and AIDS among Hispanics

The 178,233 African Americans living with AIDS in the United States accounted for 43 percent of all people in the United States living with AIDS.

Of the 48 US children (younger than 13 years of age) who had a new AIDS diagnosis, 29 were African American.

*Since the beginning of the epidemic, African
    Americans have accounted for 40 percent of
    the estimated 944,306 AIDS cases diagnosed.
From the beginning of the epidemic through
    December 2004, an estimated 201,045 African
    Americans with AIDS died.
Planning for the Future*

*Of persons whose diagnosis of AIDS had been
    made since 1996, a smaller proportion of
    African Americans (64 percent) were alive
    after 9 years compared with American Indians
    and Alaska Natives (65 percent), Hispanics
    (72 percent), whites (74 percent), and Asians
    and Pacific Islanders (81 percent).*

Source: Centers for Disease Control, "Fact Sheet: HIV/AIDS Among
African Americans", 1 Feb 2006.

When I was growing up it was strong community
interaction, our own personal policing of bad behavior
and our refusal to make out of wedlock "shackin"
acceptable that provided a solid platform to teach by
example, and control the passing of sexually
transmitted diseases. Even in the 60s and 70s with free
love and smoking weed, our debt would not be paid
with the lives of our young people. In the state of Texas
there are communities where high schools are testing
positive at 50% or more. There is no future in that. Even
the jail trail will not decimate our communities at that
level.

The solution is for us to take responsibility for our own behavior. We must stop talking about the problem and solve it. My generation seriously failed the current generation. We chose to be their friends instead of parents and grandparents. The challenge that Mother dear left us was a challenge of responsibility to our young people.  In 1954 she wrote for Ebony magazine the following words:

*"The world around us really belongs to youth for youth will take over its future management. Our children must never lose their zeal for building a better world. They must not be discouraged from aspiring toward greatness, for they are to be the leaders of tomorrow. Nor must they forget that the masses of our people are still underprivileged, ill-housed, impoverished and victimized by discrimination. We have a powerful potential in our youth, and we must have the courage to change old ideas and practices so that we may direct their power toward good ends."*

My generation has allowed the "zeal" of our youth to be lost and replaced by an over arching desire for "respect". Not the kind that is earned through good deeds and worthy causes but the kind that is generated through fear, gaining cool points for executions of innocent people and jail time.

We must move to a position of being responsible for mentoring as well as raising our own to reach the greatness within. Even in the face of double digit unemployment, gas prices that are criminal and the ever rising cost of day to day living, the opportunity to regain what has been lost is greater than ever.

When I read the words of my grandmother, written in 1954 and yet so very relevant to the issues we face today, it is so very clear that she was a forward thinker and understood the greatness that lies within our community. From the first enslaved African that arrived in this country, the intention of the enslaver was never for us to survive this long. We were to parish when our usefulness was no longer perceived as necessary. Yet, through all the attempts to destroy us, we have survived. Not only have we survived but we have achieved at the highest levels in spite of the incredible obstacles placed before us. We have made it possible for a nation to reach higher heights than ever thought possible and much of the great strides to international greatness came on the backs of our ancestors.

We cannot be so careless as to destroy ourselves from within by forgetting the price that was paid for us to live. We have endured the worst holocaust in the history of the world and yet managed to produce greatness such as Langston Hughes, Dr. Mary McLeod Bethune, Marcus Garvey, Dorothy Height, Ida b. Wells, Dr. Cornel West, Dr. James Conyers, Samuel and Patsy McLeod and the millions of unknown Africans who bled and died so we could live. When my grandmother found her freedom from sharecropping she insured that others who would come after her would not have to be share croppers but have the same opportunity as every other citizen. Could there have been an Oprah if there had not been a Mary McLeod Bethune? Were there no Oprah, would there be a Tracy Boyd of Nascence Media Group?

I know that there would not be an Evelyn Bethune if there had not been Samuel and Patsy McLeod or an Albertus and Mary McLeod Bethune and for sure an Albert and Elizabeth Bethune. Our children suffer today because we have forgotten the value of our history. We do not call the names of our ancestors and welcome their presence, their protection and most of all their wisdom. We are in disarray because we forgot how a people who were liberated but given nothing but the rags on their backs managed to reach the state houses and the White House. They never thought that they couldn't achieve which is why they could. We must regain the lost legacies and teach our children so that they will always be prepared and eager to learn.

Mary McLeod Bethune said that education is the key to freedom and that without it one will always be in shackles. I don't know everything but what I know is that the strength of my people is beyond the human and into the super natural; it is a gift from God and should never be taken for granted.

Many of my friends ask why I am always around young people. It is because they are always trying new things. They are curious and willing to try. If they fail they must be encouraged to try again. My daddy used to tell us that his job was not done until we were successful. I know that he is watching over me because I am not successful yet. I still fall down and I make mistakes but because of what he placed in me I never stop trying. I never give up. Sometimes I get tired, sometimes I am discouraged but it is in those times that I am closest to God and to my ancestors. It is their strength that lifts me and it will be my strength that will lift others.

I am so very encouraged when I go to book fairs and literary Salons like the one held during the National Black Arts Festival 2008 and I see young people buying books and writing books. They are asking questions and their creativity is deep and wide. They give me the strength to climb.

# "This Little Light of Mine, I'm Gonna Let It Shine"

All of us have people in our lives that have cut a path for us. That path finder for me was my grandson Charles. He is the reason that I have pushed so hard to get this book finished. I want him to have a foundation to stand on that is stable and reassuring. I want him to be free to laugh and dream his dreams, knowing that dreams do come true.

It is his unconditional love for me that has made me able to face my demons. Throughout his life he has always been quick to smile and not too anxious to be older than he is. He will make time to talk to me when I call him and every now and then he will e-mail or text me. He is so full of love that I dread the day he falls in love with the wrong person so I try to "drop knowledge" on him every chance I get. I may not be able to prevent it but maybe I can slow it down. He gives totally honest answers so if you don't want to know don't ask him. When he says "grandma, I love you", nothing could be more valuable to me.  I thank God for everything.

The names of my Grandmothers brothers and sisters are:
Samuel, Satira, Julia, Rebecca, Sally, Kissie, Kelly, Carrie, Beauregard, Cecelia, Magdalena, Mattie Bell, William Thomas, Hattie, Mazie and Monday . . .
Mary was the light for them.
Call their names so that they may never be forgotten.

## Others who shine light:

Massoud Nayeri

Melinda Iley Dohn

Cherry Steinwender

Dr. Trudie Reed

Marcia Bethune Johnson

Charles Miller, Jr.

Elizabeth V. Bethune

Hobson Bethune

Robert Bethune

Sara Bethune-Smith

Jarvis Smith

Christopher Harold

LeNard Harold

Nicky Bethune

Justin Bethune

Toi Washington

Tori Scarborough

Dr. Leonard L. Favorite

Pyramid Global

Barber Scotia College

President  David Olah

Rev. A. Kim McTillmon

Selvyn McTillmon

A. L. Fleming

Rev. Cleo Lamkin

Pacifica Foundation/Network

Bethune-Cookman University

Evelyn Bethune

Judy Seal

Rev. Pernell Hill

Alfred Green

Ms. Eddie Mae Stevens

**President Barack Obama**

**First Lady Michelle Obama and**

**Malia and Sasha Obama**

    ***And many, many others…***

*Who shines the light for you and for whom are you shining your light?*

The Pacifica Network includes five sister stations in New York, Washington DC, Los Angeles, Berkeley, and Houston along with many affiliated independent radio stations throughout the United States.
Pacifica broadcasts via satellite and Internet and have one of the most extensive and important sound archives in the world. The Network is energizing independent community radio through collaboration, interactivity and program exchange throughout the network

Pacifica Foundation.org

Pacifica.org

Radio For Peace

The Essence of Woman

FAITH

*Give her of the fruit of her hands: and let her own works praise her in the gates.*
The Indianapolis Section of NCNW

Ms. Clem Lewis Turner, First Vice President,   Dr. Mollie A. Williams, General Chair, Dr. Evelyn Bethune, Recipient of the Bethune Achiever Award 2008,  and Mrs. Dorothy Allen Chimney, Texas State Convener—NCNW

It is good to
LAUGH

The
Mary McLeod Bethune
Educational Legacy
Foundation, Inc.
Atlanta  Annual Board
Meeting

The
Mary McLeod Bethune
Educational Legacy
Foundation, Inc.
Atlanta  Annual Board
Meeting

Lafayette Harris Jr and Janine Brooks

Bethune Twins—Robert and Hobson, Sr.

Lafayette Harris Jr. at the Grand

The
Mary McLeod Bethune
Educational Legacy
Foundation, Inc.
Atlanta Board Meeting.

# *Reflections of*

# *Family, Friends &*

# *Mentor*

## *In their own words...*

# Family

# Reflections

## *Hobson Sr.'s Reflections*

Being the grandson of Dr. Mary McLeod Bethune gave me a special vantage point in my prospective on life, I think quite unique. My twin brother Robert and I were born exactly 9 months after our grandmother's passing. A significance that I share with my little brother, expressed as being conceived while my father, Albert McLeod Bethune Sr. was consoled by my mother, Elizabeth Sterricks Bethune, during his mourning the death of his mother. The timetable of those two events, her death and our conception, gave us the comfort of a unique connection, since we weren't around during her amazing life. To many I suppose, it was amazing too, when you take into consideration that our Dad was 56 years old at the time.

Our childhood was very special too, due to the fact that although we were not blessed with a whole lot of money, we had more than enough love. In fact, there was so much love in our household, most of my friends growing up, spent more time at our house than their own. My mother was a beautician and had her shop at the house. I can recall Robert and I having a band during our early teen years and we practiced in our bedroom, which was right next to Mom's beauty shop. There was even a window between the rooms. The noise of several youths playing instruments as loud as they could never disturbed our Mother and I never heard a complaint from any of her customers either. And trust me; it wasn't because of the beautiful music that filled the air.

Our home was like a recreation center where all of our friends were welcome, and treated like they belonged. Both my Mother and Father had hearts big enough to take in all the kids in the neighborhood and care for anybody that needed.  After graduation from high school I joined the United States Marines on a two year enlistment planning to go on to college afterwards. Well, that two year enlistment turned into a 28 year career, taking me all over the world, meeting many great and interesting people and doing things it would take more time than I have to tell you about.  My brother Robert and sister's, Evelyn and Sara, can tell you of the love we shared at home with our beloved parents, whom both have passed on to greater glory.

I lived the life of a Marine to the fullest and took care of my Marines the best I could while raising my own two sons, Hobson II and Rashad.  The oldest, Hobson II, a graduate of Albany State University now pursuing a corporate career with AT & T, recently accepting a new position in Ohio. My youngest is back in college after finishing a tour in the U.S. Marines. I am so proud of my sons, as they are both growing into responsibly, respectful men, aware of and concerned about the world around them.

During my travels all over the world there was never a location where my grandmothers' accomplishments were not known. We have a saying in the Marines, "It's hard to be humble, when you're the worlds finest". But I've been quite humbled personally in my travels, by the respect of so many people, of all races, of my dear grandmother, Dr. Mary McLeod Bethune. The founder of a thriving university, one of her favorite projects among many; so important even today, as we struggle for equality in higher education in a country now facing the possibility of its first black president, but has yet to take full responsibility for the atrocities committed against African American people.

As I take all of this in and fathom the thought of my sister Evelyn finishing her book, many things have become clearer. The trials we endure and overcome make us what we are. My sister has experienced more than one human should have to endure, but because of the same kind of faith that ran through the hand, heart and head of my grandmother, "Ma Dear", she has persevered, now preparing to finish probably her greatest work. As part of her works I wanted to be included as her brother, supporting all that she does, because I know where her heart is and the fact that she has the talent to do anything she wants.

As the grandson of Dr. Mary McLeod Bethune I always felt an obligation to do the right thing and care about others, even before myself. Rising up the ladder while in the Marines reaching the rank of Master Gunnery Sergeant, I also chose to work with at-risk youth coordinating the Drug Education for Youth Program (DEFY). I mention this to say that I am not surprised at Evelyn's accomplishment in regard to her writing this book. I also understand how important it is for my sister to know how proud I am of her. Most of our adult life I've been away in the Marines, only touching base at home occasionally at reunions and holidays. We've stayed in touch over the years via phone or email and now getting closer as many of us are moving back home. In this book Evelyn wanted each of our input on our feelings as grandchildren of Dr. Mary McLeod Bethune. Well I could write a book myself but to put into some form Evelyn could use I've tried to summarize my life to some degree to illustrate the impact of my grandmother on my life.

I didn't realize the magnitude of her contributions and recognition internationally until my travels around the world as a Marine. That recognition has always driven me to perform well, always feeling that "Ma Dear" was watching and nodding approval at my successes. I can perhaps sum this up with this little story. During my youth I spent a great amount of time on the campus of Bethune-Cookman University and ran in and out of one of the campus's main buildings, "White Hall" which had a sign above the entrance that read "Enter to Learn, Depart to Serve". I must have read that sign a million times as a kid and later found that to be my calling even though I never actually attended BCU as a student. In other words, I came to know my grandmother's contribution over a period that extended beyond my youth and well into my career as a Marine. Her desire to serve her people is part of my heritage and a driving force in my work as well. I'm now living in

Daytona Beach again and working as the Executive Director of the Police Athletic League working with at-risk youth. The impressions from my grandmother, ingrained in my spirit are to "Learn continuously, and then teach passionately. Teach one, Reach One".

## Robert's Reflections

This is an open letter from **Robert McLeod Bethune**. Its purpose is two-fold in that I'll try to tell how I feel about being a Bethune as well as tell how I feel about my sister Evelyn ( I like referring to her as Doctor Evelyn Bethune when I'm talking about her) and her publishing a book (finally) on that same subject. I was asked to be concise and to the point so here goes....Of all the places I've been, people I've encountered, situations and circumstances I've been in my life. I would have to say the hardest has been simply being *"A Bethune."*

In my personal experience, growing up as a grand-child, of Dr. Mary McLeod Bethune, offered no obvious advantages. Our parents were not wealthy and this was a disadvantage only because most of my friends either thought we were or figured we should have been. There was however, a lot of love so there was some balance. Growing up I could feel the negativity from the college administration towards us as a family, and as a result I personally developed ambivalent feelings for the college itself and sometimes I resented being a Bethune altogether. Many times when I reflect on decisions I've made, I felt that had I come from another family I would have more fully used my God-given talent and potential to reach some higher goals in life. But I rest assured that if I leave this world today, I have not wasted the most important thing we as a family got from our grandmother, and that was a desire to help others. No matter how I might have felt about the college and how my family may or may-not have been treated, there was always an inner pride that we as a family felt that no one on the outside could destroy, which leads me to my sister, Evelyn.

Since our parents passed she has been the spiritual leader of this family, and in my opinion, has embodied the essence of our Grandmother. A brilliant and gifted speaker, she has always worked for the people of her community. Sometimes, I've felt, to her disadvantage. "Putting others first, is the curse," of being Bethune, is what I sometimes call it.

## Sara's Reflections

Growing up Bethune was and is a life I would not change in many ways and then there are some things I wish I could take back. But that's life and we all wish we could do some things differently in our past.

As a child I can say that I didn't truly understand what it meant to be the granddaughter of the great Dr. Mary McLeod Bethune. My childhood was like all of my friends', filled with school and playing. I was lucky, in that I had the whole campus as my play ground, from one building to the next. I had lots of aunts and uncles. Though I was born after the death of my grandmother, many of the people in my life were alive during her life time so I had the wonderful stories my family and especially my father told me about Mother Dear. Daddy had hundreds of stories that no one knew but him and his father. There have been many who claim to know all but they don't and never will. Yes Dr. Bethune was a Great woman no one can ever say she wasn't.

As I grew older I had to learn the hard stuff about life and people and how nasty they could be. To have teachers in school not see me but only my grandmother and what she did. I was always expected to do well and do as she did but it only made it harder to be me. I played in school a lot and my grades were not my number one goal at the time. What I wanted more than anything was to just be accepted for my own qualities, not just seen as the granddaughter of Dr. Mary McLeod Bethune. I was not always sure what I wanted to be or do but what I did know was I wanted to help people as she did. I just didn't know how back then.

To me the worst part of it all was how some people treated my father after his mother died. He was pushed aside and over looked by many who have since passed. People that he helped when they had a need, when he was younger and financially able, chose ego and position over keeping the promises made of ensuring the care of the only offspring of Dr. Mary McLeod Bethune. Greed is one of the seven deadly sins and it can cause people to commit terrible wrongs. Some who are still here and never tried to right all the wrongs they committed to him and his children will hopefully read this book and know that words as well as deeds matter in the eyes of God. We all have been through some things good and bad because of what we saw growing up. Some of us almost died behind it all. I still cry some times for my parents and my sister and brothers. I still carry it all in my heart.

Once I was on campus and was told by a staff member that just because my last name was Bethune didn't mean a thing to her. The assumption that I was looking for favoritism was incorrect, and the hostility she showered me with was felt deeply. That was years ago but still true to this day I believe with all my heart that we are not welcomed on those hallowed grounds called Bethune-Cookman College/University. Many of us have tried to make ourselves apart of B-CU, not for money, not for frame as some believe but because we were told it was our right and responsibility to help keep her dream alive the way our father told it to us. We were never given that chance and for so many wrong reasons. We were kept distant by people who yet today, have no clue what any of us are truly about in our spirits and souls. So few have ever taken the time to even ask or hear.

We were raised by proud parents who worked very hard to give us the best life they could and for that I have been blessed by God. If I could have one wish before my time is up on this earth, it would be for Mary's Grandbabies to all take their place on campus, if they so desire, each doing what they can to keep the family dream alive because one cannot go on without the other no matter how hard some try to keep us out. We all have to come home because it was our blood that broke the ground. It was our sweat that laid the bricks one by one and it is our spirit and love that will truly bless all who enter those doors.

*Peace and Blessings to all who feel my words.*
Sara Bethune-Smith,
*Granddaughter of the Great Mary McLeod Bethune, a black woman of which to be proud*

P.S.
Evelyn I hope my words are what you needed for your book and I hope you have many blessings because of it.

# Great-Grands Speak

## Elizabeth's Reflections

I am sitting at the gravesite of my great grandmother, known to the world as Dr Mary McLeod Bethune, but to our family as *Mother Dear*. Looking around at my fellow classmates as we prepare for graduation honors, I am continually amazed how a woman, a black woman, the descendant of former slaves and the first one of her 16 siblings born free, created this opportunity for me and others. She willed this opportunity out of her spirit, out of her undying thirst for knowledge and justice. In graduating from Bethune-Cookman College I realize, finally, that the journey is just beginning.

I may never know what took me so long to appreciate and value her sacrifices but I am grateful that I finally felt her spirit in me. How dare I come from such greatness and choose to live in mediocrity, to live a life of self-servitude? The mere thought that I can choose to be educated is a blessing all in itself. I have come to understand that being average means being the best of the worse and the worse of the best. My great grandmother set the tone for greatness and I have her genes in me. I had to understand what that meant before I was open enough to meet the challenge. Today, I am open to the possibilities.

After ten years of procrastination and avoidance, I finally heard her in my thoughts and spirit. I heard her speak to me; I saw the gifts she laid before me. I listened and I took action. I had to come to my senses to accept my gift and not be afraid of my cross to bear that comes with service to others. I completed my Criminal Justice Degree during the 100 year anniversary of Bethune-Cookman College as a member of the first class to receive their degree from a woman president, since Dr. Bethune retired as the head of Bethune-Cookman College in 1947. Dr. Trudie Kibbie Reed stated that this was a historical moment for the college, but it is also a defining moment in my life. I had completed what I started and I knew that *Mother Dear* would be proud. But I also knew the race was just beginning and I was still thirsty.

In the Last Will and Testament of Dr. Mary McLeod Bethune, she states that she leaves us a "thirst for knowledge". Approaching my graduation date left me feeling parched because *my thirst* grew stronger, the thirst she always talked about... *Mother Dear* placed within us the thirst for knowledge. She was right when she stated, in the 1930s, that *"knowledge is forever and will always be the key to freedom".* My desire is now stronger, and a new thirst parches my mind and will only be quenched by a consumption of knowledge. I know that I have to reach for the high ground and prepare for the challenges ahead for there is a great need in my community for sincere leadership, mentors for the next generation and role models who are not afraid to shine light in the dark places. That was the example left to me by my great grandmother and the need today is as strong as it was 100 years ago, if not greater.

My wish is the wish of my great grandmother that I continue to grow and strive for excellence in everything that I do. Not for my sole benefit but for the betterment of those that come behind me. Let me clear a path so others may have a safer journey. I eagerly "Enter to learn, depart to serve" as I go forward as Dr. Mary McLeod Bethune did, "not for myself but for others."

She believed that if every person would just do their part to make the world a place of peace and equality for everyone, we would achieve our dreams. Her dream is now my dream. Just as an Olympic torchbearer passes the torch until eventually it lights the eternal flame, I too carry a light, a fire ignited from the eternal flame of knowledge, perseverance, achievement and service. I want to do my part.

*"Faith is the first factor in a life devoted to service. Without it, nothing is possible. With it, nothing is impossible."*
*Mary McLeod Bethune (1875 - 1955)*
*Educator/Activist/Dreamer*

## Marcia's Reflections

I'm really not sure if any words can possibly express how proud I am to be Mary McLeod Bethune's great granddaughter.  The enormity of that fact almost escapes me in my everyday life.  However, when I sit back and think about all the great things she accomplished, I am still astonished.  There was not a "how to" book for her to follow or even an individual to show her the way.  My great grandmother was simply placed on this Earth to be great!  She had it in her heart to ensure that our people had the tools they needed to live better.

My great grandmother loved the business of producing strong, educated, and ethically correct individuals to carry our community.  It's not hard to understand why she was and still is loved by so many.  My great grandmother's entrepreneurial spirit runs through my veins just as her blood does.  Not only do I know how she took nothing and made it into something, crossed unimaginable hurdles to reach her goals, and never ever took "NO" as the final answer... I feel it.  Through her unwavering love of God, she learned early in life that to honor Him and His word, you must do what your heart tells you.  I believe that God guides us and communicates with us through our hearts.  The reason that we can all look at Bethune Cookman University with extreme pride is due to my great grandmother listening to God... through her heart.

Being a business woman myself, I often have obstacles to overcome. Sometimes I may even wonder if I have the strength to continue. This feeling never lasts long because I think about my lineage. Thoughts of my great grandmother Mary, my grandmother Elizabeth, my grandfather Albert Sr., and my mother Evelyn strengthen me. Just the thought of them gives me the resilience to continue on my mission to be successful not only in business, but also as a person.

Mommy..... I'm so very proud of you. I know that this book was truly a labor of love for you. Thank you for sharing your story.

## Reflections of Hobson II

Hello all, my name is **Hobson McLeod Bethune II** and I am the proud Great-Grandson of Dr. Mary McLeod Bethune. It has been an interesting experience growing up being a direct descendant of such a powerful and positive person in our history. I think back to my childhood and remember having thoughts "no one cares" what she did for us, or people saying "ya'll must got money". Neither is true in a sense.

My family was pretty normal you could say. My father served 28 years in the United States Marine Corps, one brother in college and served in the Marine Corps reserves, and my mother works in the medical field (not a doctor though...). My family was not perfect, but we all love each other through tough and good times.

There were times when I would have conversations with people and Mary's name would come up and I would think to my self "damn, her blood is standing here right in front of them and they have no clue". I really wasn't big on broadcasting to the world what I was a part of. I felt people would either think I was lying or bragging. I pretty much kept it to myself. However, if someone heard something from a 3rd party and approached me with the question: "are you related to Mary McLeod Bethune". It would open the flood gates. I would go into detail of some of the things she has accomplished for us as Black people in this country down to the "Classic" football games I had the opportunity to attend in Orlando (Bethune Cookman vs. FAMU). Other than that, I made it a necessity to conduct myself as a normal person amongst the rest.

At this very moment, my aunt (Dr. Evelyn Bethune) is in the process of getting this book "Mary's Grandbabies" together on behalf of Mary Bethune and the rest of the family. It feels good to see our family finally coming together for something that is not a death or something else negative. This is a grand opportunity to show our people that her struggle still exists and we all need to play our part in elevating the state of Blacks in not only America, but the world as a whole. This book will reach and open the eyes of some demographics of our society that may not have knowledge of her legacy. Particularly, our Black women in this country need to take a close look at what Mary went through in order for them to have most of the opportunities available for them today.

We are now caught up in a materialistic, fast-paced environment. It's ok to have a good time, but, in moderation. Our people tend to focus on the wrong things at times or look up to negative behavior. That's not right. We need to reevaluate our perspectives and live as the true intelligent kings, queens, princes, and princesses that we are. This is a big step in the right direction for our family and I'm excited to see its impact.

# Jarvis Reflects

Dear Aunty Evelyn,

Today my heart is filled with great joy as I take a moment to celebrate you and your newest accomplishment. I recently learned about the completion of your first book, entitled *"BETHUNE: Out of Darkness into the Light of Freedom"*

Truly, this has been a long-awaited project that could only be written by few. Aunty, I'm very excited in so many ways to see one of your biggest dreams come to life which has inspired me much as a young entrepreneur. I want you to know that as you launch out into deep waters of faith, know that I will always support your dreams both far and near. I'm very proud to be your nephew. In my understanding there is a time and a season for all things. It is my greatest belief that God has chosen you to rejuvenate the life, the legacy, and the honor of our grandmother that has been forgotten locally and nationally by many.

As a child, of the younger generation of the Bethune family I was not fortunate to meet my great-grandmother. I've heard many stories of great accomplishments in addition to photos of people of elite status and awards from many different organizations. Again, I'm very proud to be apart of a legacy that has and will continue to enhance lives through the various types of avenues established by my great-grandmother.

In conclusion, it is my sincere hope that this book will not only expose the life of our great-grandmother and her passion to many who have unanswered questions but also give a glimpse into the lives of those who are her rightful heirs. Mary McLeod Bethune left a living legacy, a family filled with her spirit of service to community and unselfish giving. This book will be a beacon of light for multiple generations to come.

*Surely this will be a best seller! Humbly Submitted,*
*Jarvis M. Smith, Great-Grandson of the late, Dr. Mary McLeod Bethune*

# The Great-Great Grands

## Reflections of Charles "CJ" Miller, Jr.

My Grandma E, I love so much. She is like a second mother but always staying my grandma. She always spoiled me even though they told her don't. She is like one of my best friends but teaches me new things nobody else can. We also have our off and on moments but they never last long because we love each other so much. I can go to her about anything and I know she would do anything she could for me. She helps me with my attitude because I and everyone else know it needs a lot of work. She keeps me motivated to do good when others aggravate me into giving up on everything. I know with her helping me I can accomplish anything.

To be Mary's great-great grandson is amazing. I never had the chance to meet her but its just amazing just to know that somebody in our family came from $1.50 to founding a collage and so many other things. It's so amazing that when I tell people they don't even believe me, but I know she's my great- great grandma...and that's all that matters. The reactions and facial expressions on some people's faces are priceless. Sometimes I have the urge to say I'm just the great – great grandson but I know to some people that it is a really big deal to meet me. So I guess I could say it's pretty interesting to have this title.

My Grandma E believes in never giving up and she shows me and a lot of other people how being persistent pays off. Other young people like being around her too because she lets us be ourselves but tries to tell us how to be better in a way we understand. She has worked on this book for a long time and even when no one else was helping her get it done, she kept doing it and now it is ready to go. She never gave up. She has taught me that you should never give up on your dreams and so I am going to college at Bethune-Cookman University, started by my great-great grandmother so I can realize my dream of being a chef and owning restaurants. I am really proud of my grandma and my great-great grandma.

Love ya grandma,

CJ

## Reflections of Ms. Bookecia T. Williams

I remember as a child growing up going to different ceremonies honoring my great-great grandmother Dr. Mary McLeod Bethune. People would greet us with sincere admiration. We received royal treatment. However, when we attend various ceremonies in Daytona Beach, the home of Dr. Bethune, the atmosphere is totally different. It seemed as if my family had to be our own support system because we were there to honor our grandmother, no matter what.

I remember always being proud of my grand aunt Evelyn. She was always chosen to represent the family with a wonderful speech. After all she has the credentials, intellect, and beauty to speak on behalf of our family anyday. My family has done their share of showing the world that Dr. Bethune still has living, willing, and able descendants to carry on her legacy. However, we continue to be mistreated, ignored, and looked down upon.

Why is it that friends and family members of Bethune-Cookman University have been able to attend for free? Immediate family members only get half off of their tuition. Shouldn't that be the other way around? We have been promised football tickets and had to scatter at the last minute to purchase them because our tickets where sold. Do you know how that made us feel as a family; the only ones to be left out of everything, when in reality we should be the first to be given consideration?  After all, Mother Dear already paid the cost.

Why was the National Youth Sports Program discontinued?  That program gave our children a safe haven in the summertime.  The program provided meals, physical fitness, and a positive environment. Children from Daytona Beach, Deland, New Smyrna and all surrounding areas were in attendance.  Those children were future wildcats!

B-CU was founded in 1904.  To my knowledge there has never been an immediate family member employed at the University.  In April of 2008, I was offered a job in the Office of Admissions.  Upon accepting the position, I was advised that the department really did not want to hire me because I was a member of the Bethune family. However, they where encouraged by a close family friend who is employed at the University to, "give it a try."  What had me so baffled is the fact that I was discriminated against from the day I entered the doors. I knew this, and went to work everyday and gave it my all.  My productivity report was always above average and I did more than what was asked of me.  I was not seeking special recognition, but trying to prove that I am here to work no matter who I am related to.  In spite of all my efforts, I continued to be mistreated and talked down to.  The University was successful! I would rather leave with pride than stay and be fired because I said something inappropriate.  I was told the reason the University never wanted a family member to be employed there is because they did not want someone who was really concerned to get a whiff of their financial mishaps.

In 2001, I received my Bachelor of Science degree from B-CU. Upon receiving my degree, I had passed all levels of the CLAST test, defended my senior paper, and passed all exit exams, when the registrars' office informed me that I was supposed take Freshman Seminar upon being accepted at the University. I was told by my academic advisor that I was exempt from taking the class. Can you imagine having to take Freshman Seminar as a graduating senior? I was very upset and discouraged at that point. Once that was complete, they hit me with another stumbling block. The University told me that my reading grade from the junior college was not transferrable. Why was this not brought to my attention before then? The reading department gave me an exam to take and my graduation was contingent upon me passing. I had no time to prepare. Why was I put through so much when I worked so hard as a single parent to receive my degree? I did graduate with my class inspite of it all, with the help of my wonderful God.

In closing, these are the many questions left unanswered for my family but common to all of us is... "What have we done to be so mistreated??"

# Friends and Mentors

## Reflections of Hubert C. "Blackjack" Jackson

I feel extremely privileged having grown up in the shadow of then Bethune-Cookman College, now Bethune-Cookman University - you go BCU. I also had the privilege to witness the institution grow from a small school with a vocational division, which was designed to train returning black GIs from WWII, to a university that has engulfed several blocks in all directions of what used to be businesses and property that was cleared by the infamous Urban Renewal Project that ripped the heart out of a thriving support system for the school.

BCU has always been a community oriented school, and it remains so today. When I was growing up, Oak Street, the street on which I spent my first sixteen years of life, was dirt (that fact alone makes me three days older than dirt). I make mention of that nugget to highlight the fact that B-CC was the safest, unrestricted location that we had to break in our new Christmas Union 5 skates, and we had access to each and every sidewalk on campus! I also loved to skate on campus because B-CC was renowned for having some of the most beautiful young ladies that I have ever seen. I am surprised that I did not kill myself looking back as I would pass one on the sidewalks, but I was adapt at skating backwards!

B-CC's athletic field served as the location for the annual carnival that would come to town each year, and also served as the gathering place for the mini Boy Scout Jamborees where local and invited black Boy Scout troops would gather to test and display their skills. Another attribute that Cookman lent to the community is the interaction that the college's staff had within the community. My very first scout master, and a major mentor who made immense contributions to shaping my life, was Dr. W.A. McMillion, then the Dean of Men at B-CC. Even though his duties kept him very busy, and he had a family to rear, assisted by his very capable and lovely wife, Dr. McMillion made always himself available to lead and mentor his young men.

During the summer of my junior year in high school B-CC was the location of a summer school that was designed to introduce junior and senior level high school students, from all over the state of Florida and several other states, to college structure which involved classes as well as living in the dorms on campus with the college students, and eating in the dinning facility - for that summer we were college students, and we enjoyed every minute of that experience.

Unlike my classmates, some of whom enrolled in B-CC, after completing high school I pursued a career in the US Army. Three-quarters of the way through my military career I experienced a break in service. Having completed my associate degree while on active duty, this break proved to be a most fortuitous event in my life because it presented me with an opportunity to complete my bachelor's degree at B-CC. When I walked across the stage in Moore's Gymnasium all of the events that I spoke of earlier came rushing back to me, having seen the great lady, Dr. Mary McLeod Bethune on campus, and lying in state in her coffin in her home on campus, although I was only five years old at that time - see, I am not as old as you thought that I was - skating on campus, spending many wonderful hours at the carnival on the athletic field, the carnival atmosphere of the homecoming celebrations during the football season, and now here I was receiving my BA degree from the school that has, in one way or another, always been a very important part in my life, the school that was founded with five little girls, her 5 year old son and $1.50, and tremendous faith in God, to provide a quality education to what has come to be thousands of not only black young men and women, but young men and women of numerous races and nationalities, the school that has advanced from a small, predominately black college to a university, may God continue to bless and keep you Bethune Cookman University.

Hubert C. Jackson, Summer Class of 1990

## Janine's Reflections

What a perfect time in my life to reflect and pay tribute to a legend. There are many strong African American women who have contributed to my success. Today I would like to acknowledge one in particular; Mrs. Mary McLeod Bethune. I would also like to embrace all women of color and celebrate their inner beauty and strength.

I was inspired by Mary McLeod Bethune at the tender age of eight. It is such a vivid memory. Life begins and ends with knowledge. I was at a very inquisitive stage in my life. While in my school library I came across a story about a lady who made pies to provide education for young girls of color. I was very moved by her acts of selflessness and at that very point Mary McLeod Bethune planted a seed of love in my heart.

The life and story of Mary McLeod Bethune is filled with compassion, dedication and love. As I read each page of the story I became motivated to achieve. I felt a strong since of pride. I felt a strong connection with a lady I only knew through the pages of a story. I was amazed by her ability to channel her energy and talent to create revenue to start an institution of higher learning. Today I am a successful wife, mother, business owner, community activist and a published author.

I accept the love Mary McLeod Bethune offered, she

prayed we would have hope, faith and confidence to move forward even in the face of adversity, I accept this challenge and I vow not to forget our young people. In closing I thank Mary McLeod Bethune for the legacy that lives on based on her contribution to this society.

Janine Brooks-Collier

## Billena's Reflections

As a child learning about Dr. Mary McLeod Bethune I never even knew the caliber of woman she was, let alone how I could even compare. She was married, had a child, and then was left by her husband to raise a child as a single parent, and still opened up a Negro school for girls. Mary McLeod Bethune made a personal choice that instead of submitting to self pity she took every kick in life as a boost. In life we are faced with so much adversity God used her storm to show women like myself that you can push through. Dr. Bethune is an inspiration to every woman of color and because of women like her she made it possible for women like me to strive in today's society. Dr. Bethune didn't have nearly the opportunities afforded to her as I have now. She has inspired me to go back to school and reach back to lift up the next person.

One of my favorite quotes of hers is *"Faith is the first factor in a life devoted to service. Without it, nothing is possible. With it, nothing is impossible."* This statement yet simple outline the motto that every woman in America should adopt. Dr. Bethune has made a huge impact on my life she defied adversity in a time when women of color were not looked upon as equals at all. She has inspired me to move forward with my education and start a non – profit organization to help women with children much like her school for training Negro girls. I want to show single mothers that there is help out there.

Dr. Bethune embraced her heritage as a Black American woman, stretched the boundaries, and became a legend in her own right. The black woman has come a long way and we can attribute much of our success to pioneers before us such as Dr. Mary McLeod Bethune. Thank you to the McLeod Bethune family for sharing her with the world and keeping her memory alive.

Thank you,
Billena King Wooten

# Last Will and Testament

## Of

# Dr. Mary McLeod Bethune

## I Leave You Love

Love builds. It is positive and helpful. It is more beneficial than hate. Injuries quickly forgotten quickly pass away. Personally and racially, our enemies must be forgiven. Our aim must be to create a world of fellowship and justice where no man's skin, color or religion, is held against him. "Love thy neighbor" is a precept which could transform the world if it were universally practiced. It connotes brotherhood and, to me, brotherhood of man is the noblest concept in all human relations. Loving your neighbor means being interracial, interreligious and international.

## I Leave You Hope

The Negro's growth will be great in the years to come. Yesterday, our ancestors endured the degradation of slavery, yet they retained their dignity. Today, we direct our economic and political strength toward winning a more abundant and secure life. Tomorrow, a new Negro, unhindered by race taboos and shackles, will benefit from more than 330 years of ceaseless striving and struggle. Theirs will be a better world. This I believe with all my heart.

# I Leave You the Challenge of Developing Trust in One-Another

As long as Negroes are hemmed into racial blocs by prejudice and pressure, it will be necessary for them to band together for economic betterment. Negro banks, insurance companies and other businesses are examples of successful, racial economic enterprises. These institutions were made possible by vision and mutual aid. Confidence was vital in getting them started and keeping them going. Negroes have got to demonstrate still more confidence in each other in business. This kind of confidence will aid the economic rise of the race by bringing together the pennies and dollars of our people and plowing them into useful channels. Economic separatism cannot be tolerated in this enlightened age, and it is not practicable. We must spread out as far and as fast as we can, but we must also help each other as we go.

# I Leave You a Thirst for Education

Knowledge is the prime need of the hour. More and more, Negroes are taking full advantage of hard-won opportunities for learning, and the educational level of the Negro population is at its highest point in history. We are making greater use of the privileges inherent in living in a democracy. If we continue in this trend, we will be able to rear increasing numbers of strong, purposeful men and women, equipped with vision, mental clarity, health and education.

## I Leave You Respect for the Use of Power

We live in a world which respects power above all things. Power, intelligently directed, can lead to more freedom. Unwisely directed, it can be a dreadful, destructive force. During my lifetime I have seen the power of the Negro grow enormously. It has always been my first concern that this power should be placed on the side of human justice.

Now that the barriers are crumbling everywhere, the Negro in America must be ever vigilant lest his forces be marshaled behind wrong causes and undemocratic movements. He must not lend his support to any group that seeks to subvert democracy. That is why we must select leaders who are wise, courageous, and of great moral stature and ability. We have great leaders among us today: Ralph Bunche, Channing Tobias, Mordecai Johnson, Walter White, and Mary Church Terrell. [The latter now deceased]. We have had other great men and women in the past: <u>Frederick Douglass</u>, <u>Booker T. Washington</u>, <u>Harriet Tubman</u>, and <u>Sojourner Truth</u>. We must produce more qualified people like them, who will work not for themselves, but for others.

## I Leave You Faith

Faith is the first factor in a life devoted to service. Without faith, nothing is possible. With it, nothing is impossible. Faith in God is the greatest power, but great, too, is faith in oneself. In 50 years the faith of the American Negro in himself has grown immensely and is still increasing. The measure of our progress as a race is in precise relation to the depth of the faith in our people held by our leaders. Frederick Douglass, genius though he was, was spurred by a deep conviction that his people would heed his counsel and follows him to freedom. Our greatest Negro figures have been imbued with faith. Our forefathers struggled for liberty in conditions far more onerous than those we now face, but they never lost the faith. Their perseverance paid rich dividends. We must never forget their sufferings and their sacrifices, for they were the foundations of the progress of our people.

## I Leave You Racial Dignity

I want Negroes to maintain their human dignity at all costs. We, as Negroes, must recognize that we are the custodians as well as the heirs of a great civilization. We have given something to the world as a race and for this we are proud and fully conscious of our place in the total picture of mankind's development. We must learn also to share and mix with all men. We must make an effort to be less race conscious and more conscious of individual and human values. I have never been sensitive about my complexion. My color has never destroyed my self-respect nor has it ever caused me to conduct myself in such a manner as to merit the disrespect of any person. I have not let my color handicap me. Despite many crushing burdens and handicaps, I have risen from the cotton fields of South Carolina to found a college, administer it during its years of growth, and become a public servant in the government of our country and a leader of women. I would not exchange my color for all the wealth in the world, for had I been born white I might not have been able to do all that I have done or yet hope to do.

## I Leave You a Desire to Live Harmoniously with Your Fellow Man

The problem of color is worldwide. It is found in Africa and Asia, Europe and South America. I appeal to American Negroes -- North, South, East and West -- to recognize their common problems and unite to solve them.

I pray that we will learn to live harmoniously with the white race. So often, our difficulties have made us hypersensitive and truculent. I want to see my people conduct themselves naturally in all relationships -- fully conscious of their manly responsibilities and deeply aware of their heritage. I want them to learn to understand whites and influence them for good, for it is advisable and sensible for us to do so. We are a minority of 15 million living side by side with a white majority. We must learn to deal with these people positively and on an individual basis.

## *I leave You Finally, A Responsibility to Our Young People*

The world around us really belongs to youth for youth will take over its future management. Our children must never lose their zeal for building a better world. They must not be discouraged from aspiring toward greatness, for they are to be the leaders of tomorrow. Nor must they forget that the masses of our people are still underprivileged, ill-housed, impoverished and victimized by discrimination. We have a powerful potential in our youth, and we must have the courage to change old ideas and practices so that we may direct their power toward good ends.

Faith, courage, brotherhood, dignity, ambition, responsibility -- these are needed today as never before. We must cultivate them and use them as tools for our task of completing the establishment of equality for the Negro. We must sharpen these tools in the struggle that faces us and find new ways of using them. The Freedom Gates are half-ajar. We must pry them fully open.

If I have a legacy to leave my people, it is my philosophy of living and serving. As I face tomorrow, I am content, for I think I have spent my life well. I pray now that my philosophy may be helpful to those who share my vision of a world of Peace, Progress, Brotherhood, and love.

*Dr. Mary McLeod Bethune*

*Written for publication in Ebony Magazine 1954*

# A Glimpse of History

The African Morning Post  1954
Mary McLeod Bethune writes about
Moral- Re Armament

AFRICAN MORNING POST

REGD AT GPO AS A NEWSPAPER
F. Therson—Cofie  Editor

Phone No 4229      P O Box  217    Accra

PRICE:      ONE PENNY

Mon  Nov  22   t

# Unity Under God

## By Mrs. Mary McLeod Bethune

I AM a representative of 16 million black people in America and I think of the darker peoples of the world who have been hungering thirsting to join hands with mankind everywhere to bring about a world of peace and brotherhood and understanding

When I look back 79 years ago I see myself coming from the home life of slaves  My mother and my father were slaves in America. We were hungry and thirsting for help for light for that thing that would help us to grow and become what we believed our God wanted us to be. We wanted light intelligence we wanted that spiritual guidance that would lead us into full manhood and womanhood that could help bless the world.

How I thank God for this ideology of Moral Re Armament that has come to us So simple So all inclusive. It places the truth on the lower shelf where all of us regardless of our creed our class our colour can reach and become enriched thereof

During my years I have been an educator  Just fifty years ago now with one dollar and fifty cents faith in God and desire to serve we planted Bethune—Cookman College. There were comparatively no schools for the training of my people in that particular section There was no leadership that would guide them in the paths in which they should go

Now in my 80th year as I look back and see the thousands and thousands that my life has touched I am wanting desiring to unfold to them the real thoughts that I have found here at Caux I feel that Caux is providing us the wherewithal to unite the minds and the hearts of the peoples of the world.

This is the great centre for the meeting and the uniting of minds Here I have found no sign of segregation or discrimination

Under God we have the peoples of the world who have united their hearts and their minds in such a way that we feel as one.

# Letter to President Harry Truman

The Hon. Harry S. Truman
President of the United States
The White House
Washington, D.C.

My dear Mr. President -

We are all very mindful of you and the grave responsibility
that is yours during these days of crisis. Our thoughts and
our prayers go out, daily, that the stream of wisdom in your
fertile mind be broadened, and that your spiritual undergird-
ing be strengthened as the problems of the world claim your
decisions.

The hearts of the women of America are greatly warmed by your
appointment of Attorney Edith Sampson of Chicago, to the United
States Delegation at the United Nations. It is a step forward
that we so much desired and needed.

Your appointment of Emory Smith to the District of Columbia
judge ship was also a great encouragement to those of us who
are pitching ball with the determination that you shall always
make a home run ! Judge Hastie is another star in your sky
of appointments.

We are so happy, Mr. President, that you are drawing into
your real circle of service these strong men and women who can
and will give an account of the abilities and desires of our
minority group.

Keep on keeping on ! There are others who are waiting for your
call.

           Sincerely yours,

           Mary McLeod Bethune

Daytona Beach
Florida
August 24, 1950

## Response from President Harry Truman

THE WHITE HOUSE
WASHINGTON

August 28, 1950

Dear Mrs. Bethune:

Thank you for your kind letter of August twenty-fourth. I appreciate your thought in writing and am glad to have your generous expressions of approval.

Your prayerful remembrances in these trying days mean ever so much to me.

Very sincerely yours,

Harry Truman

Mrs. Mary McLeod Bethune,
631 Pearl Street,
Daytona Beach,
Florida.

Dr. Mary McLeod Bethune
And
THIS IS YOUR LIFE

# THIS IS YOUR LIFE

RALPH EDWARDS    .    .    HOLLYWOOD 28, CALIFORNIA

September 25th
1 9 5 2

Dear Mrs. Bethune:

Well, the show you helped build, "THIS IS
YOUR LIFE"  is taking to television.

Please SPREAD THE GOOD NEWS!   NBC-TV --
Wednesday evenings -- 10:00 p.m.  on the
Eastern cable and 10:00 p.m.  on the
Pacific coast.

Best wishes always,

Ralph Edwards

Mrs. Mary McLeod Bethune
Daytona Beach, Florida

# Dr. Mary McLeod Bethune
## And
## THIS IS YOUR LIFE

October 8, 1952

Mr. Ralph Edwards
Hollywood 28, California

My dear Ralph Edwards:

I can never forget the unforgettable night when I became the actress in "This Is Your Life." I think something happened to all of our hearts that night. I can never forget you and your secretary, your assistant, and all of those who succeeded so marvelously in keeping me in the dark until the real light appeared. I rejoice to know that your show is taking to television. Good news! Good news! It is very exciting. Do I appear in the television? I do not have a television in my house. I am going to my son's house tonight, Wednesday. He has one. The vision is not very clear here because our closest station is Jacksonville. They are to have a station here soon. But I am so excited and so happy for you, for your staff, and for all of us who participated. You were so lovely to send me a note about it. I wondered if you had forgotten me.

I was away the first part of the year. I went to Liberia. I had a wonderful stay. It was a grand experience.

Ralph Edwards, I am now building the Mary McLeod Bethune Foundation. I am taking the home in which I live as the headquarters. It will become a shrine when I am gone. My files are all being set up here. My home will be left just as I am living in it. It will be a place where people can come and get real information and inspiration, those who need it, from the living scenes of my own life. I am beginning to write my own life's story, my autobiography. "This Is Your Life" will be an exciting chapter in the story. I want this Foundation to perpetuate this house and spot as a shrine and to give out scholarships for worthy students and to afford a research place for those who may be interested in the activities of my own life.

I would like to have you Ralph, as one of our charter members. I am selecting a few people who have appreciation for my worth and my philosophy. Then we want a large number of sponsors who will be interested in helping in whatever way possible to put the funds here to carry this on and on and on. You can be of great help. Of the people in your line of work I think I love you. I think you will be happy to do this. Mrs. Roosevelt said she would be happy to participate. Have you some suggestions of some names you think I could invite, somebody who might be interested and would be helpful and who might be able to help others to help.

May I congratulate you on your success in placing this unforgettable show on television where the world might see it.

Sincerely yours,

Mary McLeod Bethune.

MMB-ww

## Dr. Mary McLeod Bethune
## And
## THIS IS YOUR LIFE

# THIS IS YOUR LIFE

RALPH EDWARDS　　·　　·　　HOLLYWOOD 28, CALIFORNIA

November 2nd
1 9 4 9

Mr. W. H. A. Carr
Publicity Director
Friends of Bethune-Cookman College
The Duane Hotel, 237 Madison Avenue
New York 16, New York

Dear Mr. Carr:

Thank you for your very wonderful letter.

I feel I may be able to help on a national
basis instead of just a West Coast basis in
the matter of Mrs. Bethune's campaign for her
college.

On the strength of the happy consequences of
several principal subject's appearances on THIS
IS YOUR LIFE, we are reporting back to our
listeners on what has been accomplished for our
principal subjects since their appearance. In
the matter of Mrs. Bethune, this might be turned
into a further plea for funds for her very worth-
while college.

Meanwhile, let me know in what manner you wish me
to assist in the formation of a West Coast Publicity
Committee to help tell the public of her efforts. I
do not guarantee that I will be able to help in this
West Coast promotion, but I will do my best and I will
be honest in telling you in what manner I can assist.

Please convey my best personal wishes to our favorite
gal, Mrs. Mary McLeod Bethune.

Sincerely,

Ralph Edwards
R
E
Z

## Dr. Mary McLeod Bethune
## And
## BARBER-SCOTIA COLLEGE

October 6, 1952

Misses Sara B. Cordery and
Mable R. Parker, Advisers
STUDENT CHRISTIAN ASSOCIATION
   Barber-Scotia College
   Concord, North Carolina

My dear Sisters:

Just the name Barber-Scotia gives to me an appreciation and a spiritual dedication that I cannot express in words. Oh, it has done so much for me. I look back to the dark days when I did not know Scotia, when I was groping in darkness and in ignorance and I contrast those days with the great light that came into my mind and into my soul when I entered Barber-Scotia. I promised my Father so sacredly that if he would only give to me a chance, that I would dedicate myself to him and to the cause of humanity and my beautiful sisters, he gave me the chance and you have only to read the story of my career, the accomplishments of my life to realize whether or not that dedication, that consecration, has produced results.

I know what candlelight ceremony at Barber-Scotia means. It lighted up my pathway in the years that have passed. It has given to me a halo of light during all of the years and I commend to you this dedication, this consecration that only comes through your faith in Jesus Christ. The world needs Christian young women like you at this time more definitely than every before. The challenge is yours. Accept it. And in this moving spiritual, inspirationa ceremony, may you, everyone of you, surrender all and let Him fill your lives and send you forth as great candlelight bearers into those darkened and benighted places where light is needed.

God bless everyone of you and make you a real blessing to others.

Your Big Sister,

Mary McLeod Bethune.

MMB-ww
Enclosures-.

## Dr. Mary McLeod Bethune
## And
## The City of Daytona Beach, FL

### The City of Daytona Beach
COMMISSION - MANAGER PLAN

DAYTONA BEACH, FLORIDA

LE ROY F. HARLOW
CITY MANAGER

March 27, 1953

Dr. Mary McLeod Bethune
631 Pearl Street
Daytona Beach, Florida

Dear Dr. Bethune:

You will recall that on September 23, 1952 we had our first conference to discuss the arrangements which would be made in keeping with the Federal District Court ruling requiring the City of Daytona Beach to provide appropriate facilities for our Negro citizens at the Peabody Auditorium. At that conference it was agreed that the arrangements made at that time were tentative, subject to review in six months to again explore the situation and see how things were going and how improvements might be made.

The six months have now expired, and I would like to suggest that we do get together as was contemplated and review the entire situation. As is so often the case, the construction program did not go as rapidly as we would have wished but progress has been made and at least we can see the work that has been done thus far.

With respect to the other arrangements which have been carried out whereby our Negro citizens and white citizens have shared enjoyment of programs in the Auditorium, it seems to me that thus far the arrangement has been as satisfactory as could be expected. I think the attitude on the part of all concerned has been one of realism and sincerity. I feel sure that there will be no change in this.

If you will let me know when your group is prepared to again meet at the Auditorium to review the situation to date and project our thinking a little ahead, we will make arrangements for the meeting.

Sincerely yours,

City Manager

T. F. LITTLE
ADMINISTRATOR

APPROVED BY
AMERICAN COLLEGE OF SURGEONS
AMERICAN MEDICAL ASSOCIATION
AMERICAN HOSPITAL ASSOCIATION

**HALIFAX DISTRICT HOSPITAL**
DAYTONA BEACH, FLORIDA
March 11, 1953.

Madam Mary MacCloud Bethune,
631 Pearl Street,
Daytona Beach, Florida.

Dear Madam Bethune:

I acknowledge the copy of your letter to Mr. J. W. Smith in connection with the matter that we discussed so thoroughly in your home a couple of weeks ago.

I am holding the copy of the letter you sent me and I will make it part of the regular agenda of the next Board Meeting of the Hospital and it will be incorporated in the minutes at that time. I am sure that you will have official acknowledgment from the Hospital.

In the meantime, let me thank you for your cooperation and with kindest regards, I remain

Very truly yours,

HALIFAX HOSPITAL DISTRICT

BY: _____
E. T. Lerren - Chairman
of the Board

TFL:js

# Dr. Mary McLeod Bethune
# And
# The Citizens Welfare League – Daytona Beach. FL

To The Members of the Executive Committee of the Citizens Welfare
League:

I make the Following Report –

1. On Saturday March 7, I received a telephone call from Mr. Lanier,
director of City Transit Service, who called me as a result of a memo-
randium sent to him by City Manager Harlow. Mr. Lanier talked with me
breifly and extended an invitation to come to his office and discussed
the bus situation. I scheduled the time and then called Rev. Summer,
Chairman of the Executive Committee, and explained to him what Mr. Lanier
had said to me. I invited Rev. Summer to join me in the visit with Mr.
Lanier.

Rev. Summer and I visited Mr. Lanier's office and we discussed at
length the bus situation, which resulted into the general agreement that
(1) the bus complaints grew out of misunderstanding. (2) the designated
official places for transfer from one bus to another are at Beach and
Volusia and at Orange and Volusia. (3) the general practice has been
that individuals coming from across the river get off the bus at the
first stop on the Mainland which is Beach and Bay. (4) the intersection
at Beach and Bay is not a transfer point and this sometimes brings about
the confusion. (a) many folk get off the bus and stop to shop at the
A & P or Piggly Wiggly and attempt to catch another bus sometimes hours
later; (b) If individuals get off the bus at Beach and Bay they should
immediatedly go up to Volusia and Beach to board another bus; (c) when the
buses stop at Beach and Bay it can only be for a very breif time since
there is no space for double parking or mass leading or unleading while
such previsions are made at the transfer points.

Mr. Lanier invited Rev. Summer or anyone designated to ride the
buses at odd hours and report on the findings to him. He furnished us
with complimentary passes. I do not know what Rev. Summers findings
will be but my findings are as follows:

1. I caught the Bus No. 8 at Madison and Ridgewood at 11:24 A.M.
Sunday March 8, and rode to the end of the line at North of U. S. 1 to
Flomich Avenue and got off at 11:30 A.M. This bus was running in an
exclusive white section driven by a white driver, I caught it at an intersection and got off where Negroes do not live. This was for the purpose
of finding out whether or not they would pick me up. The driver was court-
eous, I was comfortable, and was treated like any of the other passengers.

2. I caught Bus No. 6 on Seabreeze infront of the Atlantic Bank
at approximately 12:50 and rode the complete round – up as far as the
end of the line toward Ormond back to Orange Avenue and Beach Street at
the intersection.
I have this to report: On the corner of Seaview and Halifax
Drive, a Mr. Jackson Wilson, a Negro boarded the bus on which I was riding
on and requested a transfer on the Mainland. This made two Negroes on the
bus , I chatted with him and found that he had been coming to Daytona since
1950 with a white family, for which he works, and that the bus service has
been difficult until 1952 when he began riding any bus and not having to
wait for a Negro bus driver. He stated that it was funny how they have had
buses pass them by, waiting for a bus driven by Negroes, and that it is also
funny how the Negro hesitates to ride on a bus driven by a white driver and
and white folk do not hesitate to ride with a Negro bus driver. On the corner
of Wild Olive and Seabreeze two more passengers got on and secured a transfer
to mainland.

had said to me. I invited Rev. Summer to join me in the visit with Mr. Lanier.

Rev. Summner and I visited Mr. Lanier's office and we discussed at length the bus situation, which resulted into the general agreement that (1) the bus complaints grew out of misunderstanding. (2)the designated official places for transfer from one bus to another are at Beach and Volusia and at Orange and Volusia. (3) the general practice has been that individuals coming from across the river get off the bus at the first stop on the Mainland which is Beach and Bay. (4) the intersection at Beach and Bay is not a transfer point and this sometimes brings about the confusion. (a) many folk get off the bus and stop to shop at the A & P or Piggly Wiggly and attempt to catch another bus sometimes hours later; (b) If individuals get off the bus at Beach and Bay they should immediately go up to Volusia and Beach to board another bus; (c) when the buses stop at Beach and Bay it can only be for a very breif time since there is no space for double parking or mass loading or unloading while such provisions are made at the transfer points.

Mr. Lanier invited Rev. Summner or anyone designated to ride the buses at odd hours and report on the findings to him. He furnished us with complimentary passes. I do not know what Rev. Summners findings will be but my findings are as follows:

1. I caught the Bus No. 8 at Madison and Ridgewood at 11:24 A.M. Sunday March 8, and rode to the end of the line at North of U. S. 1 to Flomich Avenue and got off at 11:30 A.M. This bus was running in an exclusive white section driven by a white driver, I caught it at an inter-section and got off where Negroes do not live. This was for the purpose of finding out whether or not they would pick me up. The driver was court-eous, I was comfortable, and was treated like any of the other passengers.

2. I caught Bus No. 6 on Seabreeze in front of the Atlantic Bank at approximately 12:50 and rode the complete round - up as far as the end of the line toward Ormond back to Orange Avenue and Beach Street at the intersection.
I have this to report: On the corner of Seaview and Halifax Drive, a Mr. Jackson Wilson, a Negro boarded the bus on which I was riding on and requested a transfer on the Mainland. This made two Negroes on the bus , I chatted with him and found that he had been coming to Daytona since 1950 with a white family, for which he works, and that the bus service has been difficult until 1952 when he began riding any bus and not having to wait for a Negro bus driver. He stated that it was funny how they have had buses pass them by, waiting for a bus driven by Negroes, and that it is also funny how the Negro hesitates to ride on a bus driven by a white driver and and white folk do not hesitate to riding with a Negro bus driver. On the corner of Wild Olive and Seabreeze two more passengers got on and secured a transfer to mainland.

Report Continued:

I chatted with them and asked them where they transferred, and they
answered " At Beach and Bay". I went on to explain to them that
this intersection was not an official transfer point. They answered
that many get off for these reasons:

        (a) This is the first step after coming over the river.
        (b) Many get off as carry-over from the old practice.
        (c) They get off there and wait for buses driven my
           Negro drivers.
        (d) Many of them have the opportunity to run into the
           Drug store of Grocery store and shop while waiting
           so that they can catch the bus without another fare.
I then asked what would they attribute these reasons to, and they said
custom and misunderstanding.

In front of Grandview and Kare threeemore passengers got on .
I chatted with them and they informed me that they too change buses at
Bay and Beach. We went through the same discussion that I had with the
others. I asked them how long did they usually have to wait on buses
usually,.and they answered every twenty and no more than thirty minutes.
I asked if it was true on both sides and the answer I received was yes.

On the corner of Ora and Grandview two more passengers got on and
explained that they get off at Beach and Bay also. When I told them
that this was not the official transfer point, they said that they had
never been told this before. They too stated that they did not have to
wait on a bus ever twenty or thirty minutes even though they do transfer
at that point.

2. The remainder of the two days and nights I spent doing spot checking
at various intersections and places where Negroes worked across the river
and on the Mainland. I chatted with other people waiting and getting off
and on buses, in every instance I found the above statements about custom,
misunderstanding, and waiting periods were exactly the same. The folk who
work at the Sheraton Beach Hotel, can catch the bus at any time thay want to
and whatever bus they desire. Three or four persons at University and North
Halifax Drive stated the same.
    Among persons interviewed were the following: Clifford Fullword, Mrs.
Anna Gaineus, Jackson Wilson, Mrs. Armetta Hunter, Mrs. Carrie Eles, Mrs.
Georgia Woods, Miss Martha Hagan and others.

3. My overall observation is this:

    (1) A very satisfactory bus system is in operation.
    (2) Bus directors should be complimented for providing this
        additional bus service and for saving money by operating
        one Transit Company instead of two - one for Negroes and
        one for white as done in the past. Heretofore the buses
        for Negroes went over the river and came back empty behind
        a bus driven by a white driver and covering the same area
        as the other bus. This meant the two drivers had to be paid
        and expenses were needed for two buses to be operated with
        wear and tear for gas and oil included.
    (3) Now the buses can cover a larger areas and save in the oper-
        ation of the bus line.

    (4) I would recommend that we cooperate with the bus director in
        trying to get our people to transfer at the official transfer

that many get off for these reasons:
    (a) This is the first step after coming over the river.
    (b) Many get off as carry-over from the old practice.
    (c) They get off there and wait for buses driven my
        Negro drivers.
    (d) Many of them have the opportunity to run into the
        Drug store of Grocery store and shop while waiting
        so that they can catch the bus without another fare.
I then asked what would they attribute these reasons to, and they said custom and misunderstanding.

In front of Grandview and Kare threeemore passengars get on .
I chatted with them and they informed me that they too change buses at Bay and Beach. We went through the same discussion that I had with the others. I asked them how long did they usually have to wait on buses usually, and they answered every twenty and no more than thirty minutes. I asked if it was true on both sides and the answer I received was yes.

On the corner of Ora and Grandview two more passengars get on and explained that they get off at Beach and Bay also. When I told them that this was not the official transfer point, they said that they had never been told this before. They too stated that they did not have to wait on a bus over twenty or thirty minutes even though they do transfer at that point.

2. The remainder of the two days and nights I spent doing spot checking at various intersections and places where Negroes worked across the river and on the Mainland. I chatted with other people waiting and getting off and on buses, in every instance I found the above statements about custom, misunderstanding, and waiting periods were exactly the same. The folk who work at the Sheraton Beach Hotel, can catch the bus at any time they want to and whatever bus they desire. Three or four persons at University and North Halifax Drive stated the same.
Among persons interviewed were the following: Clifford Fullwood, Mrs. Anna Gaineus, Jackson Wilson, Mrs. Armetta Hunter, Mrs. Carrie Eles, Mrs. Georgia Woods, Miss Martha Hagan and others.

3. My overall observation is this:

    (1) A very satisfactory bus system is in operation.
    (2) Bus directors should be complimented for providing this additional bus service and for saving money by operating one Transit Company instead of two – one for Negroes and one for white as done in the past. Heretofore the buses for Negroes went over the river and came back empty behind a bus driven by a white driver and covering the same area as the other bus. This meant the two drivers had to be paid and expenses were needed for two buses to be operated with wear and tear for gas and oil included.
    (3) Now the buses can cover a larger areas and save in the operation of the bus line.

    (4) I would recommend that we cooperate with the bus director in trying to get our people to transfer at the official transfer points and acquaint them with the schedules.

    (5) On each bus as in other public vehicles of the South, there are these signs – "Colored Passengars seat from the rear foward and exit by the rear door" The fact that these signs are in the buses led me to believe that it was intended for Negroes to ride any or all buses.

I think that the complaints issued to us were the result of some misunderstandings.

ROBT. H. WINGFIELD
COUNTY JUDGE, VOLUSIA COUNTY
P. O. BOX 423
DELAND, FLORIDA

TELEPHONE
251

ELFRIEDA G. REHBEHN
CLERK

August 6, 1953

The Citizen's Welfare League
631 Pearl Street
Daytona Beach, Florida

    Attention Mary McLeod Bethune, President

Dear President Bethune:

    This will acknowledge receipt of your letter dated August 1, 1953 which arrived during a temporary absence of Judge Wingfield.

    This is to advise that your letter will be called to the Judge's attention immediately upon his return to the office.

          Yours very truly,

          Elfrieda G. Rehbehn
          County Judge's Clerk

EGR/bld

IN REPLY PLEASE QUOTE FILE NUMBER

*File Welfare League*

205 North Campbell Street
Daytona Beach, Florida
July 9th, 1953

Mr. Joseph E. Harris, ~~████~~,
Community Welfare League
Daytona Beach, Florida

Dear Sir:

As a businessman of the City of Daytona Beach, Volusia County,
Florida, I am writing you this letter relative to my interest as to the
teenagers of my community.

I have, since my immediate contact with the youngsters of the Community, become greatly interested in the behavior of our teenagers. I
have noticed, most frequently, between the hour of eleven (11) P. M. and
the time of my closing my place of business, which usually is around mid-
night, that there remains seated on the benches on Second Avenue a host
of boys, approximately, between the ages of 10 through 13 years of age.

My concern is of such great interest that I am asking this question,
" Is there not some way in which, you as an Organization carrying strength
and influence could abolish this policy which seems to be of a regular habit among the too-younger males of this community?".

May I, along with the older citizens of the City interested in our
boys and girls growing to be worth-while men and women of the world today
and in years to come, express our sincere greatfulness for any rod of
correction that you might endeavor to stress.

I Remain, *Philip Robinson*

*Judge Robert Wingfield*
*County Court House*
*DeLand, Fla.*

March 16, 1954

Mr. Jospeh Harris,
337 Spruce Street,
Daytona Beach, Florida.

Dear Mr. Harris:

At the last meeting of the Community Welfare League you asked that the City compile information on the cost of building sidewalk on Spruce Street between Second Avenue and Cypress Street on both sides. Also, you asked for information as to the amount of money spent out of last year's budget for street purposes in the colored section of the City.

With respect to the sidewalk cost, the sidewalks you mention would constitute 1170 lineal feet of a five foot wide sidewalk. The total cost of the East side is estimated at $2,540.00 and on the West side at $2,360.00. The City would pay 50% of the cost of such installations. As you know, the County Commissioners have indicated their willingness to pay half of the cost in some cases so you might be able to have this work done jointly by the City and County at no cost to the property owners.

With respect to the amount of money spent from our budget for streets in the colored section, our records show that the City was appropriated just under $83,000.00 for the Streets Division, including all personal services, work on paved streets, work on unpaved streets and storm sewers and drainage. The records show that $27,253.00 was spent on streets in the negro section of the City. This is about a third of the total, and is explained by the fact that there are so many unpaved streets in that area. The Public Works Director advised me, again, that approximately 90% of the City's money for street purposes last year was spent on the mainland side of the river.

I hope this is the information you desire.

REV. GEORGE O. SUMMER
CHAIRMAN EXECUTIVE COMMITTEE
251 WEAVER STREET
TELEPHONE 2-0236

VICE CHAIRMAN
CLAUDE KEYS

EXECUTIVE COMMITTEE
DR. T. A. ADAMS
REV. H. D. AVERY
C. B. CURRINGTON SR.
GEO. W. ENGRAM
REV. C. S. FELDER
JOSEPH HARRIS
RICHARD C. MCGEE
B. W. SMITH
FRANK STRICKLAND
T. D. THOMPKINS
J. H. M. WHITEHEAD

BY-LAWS CHAIRMAN
L. D. LAND

PROGRAM CHAIRMAN
H. E. HILL

ASSISTANT SECRETARY
MRS. T. E. SMALL

MAXWELL W. SAXON, SECRETARY
951 SECOND AVENUE
TELEPHONE 3-2807

T. L. SMITH, TREASURER
552 CYPRESS STREET
TELEPHONE 2-3447

# The Citizen's Welfare League

MARY McLEOD BETHUNE, PRESIDENT
631 PEARL STREET · PHONE 2-3519

## Daytona Beach, Florida
October 21, 1953

Mr. Warren Cole, President
The Civitan Club
717½ Fifth Avenue
Daytona Beach, Florida

Gentlemen:

The Citizen's Welfare League of Daytona Beach, Florida, through its Executive Committee, presents to you the name of Mrs. Mary McLeod Bethune as a nominee for the Senior Citizenship Award of the Civitan Club.

Mrs. Bethune has been a citizen of Daytona Beach for fifty years.

She founded and built the first school for higher learning in Daytona Beach.

She built and operated, for twenty years, the first hospital for Negroes in this city.

She was instrumental in bringing the first water, light and telephone lines from Ridgewood Avenue, West on Second Avenue.

Mrs. Bethune organized the first Negro Ministerial Alliance, and the first Women's Civic Club for Negroes, in Daytona Beach.

Through the medium of the Institution she founded, she organized and conducted Sunday Afternoon Community Services, presenting cultural and musical programs to the general public of this city, hence the inspiration to Mr. Peabody for the organizing and building of Peabody Auditorium.

She administered the establishment of the National Youth Administration in Daytona Beach.

She was appointed by Franklin D. Roosevelt to serve as United States Counsel in the organization of the United Nations, in San Francisco, thus representing Daytona Beach in this most important phase of international and national endeavor.

"IN UNITY THERE IS STRENGTH"

# The Citizen's Welfare League

MARY McLEOD BETHUNE, President
631 Pearl Street - Phone 2-3519

## Daytona Beach, Florida

Mr. Warren Cole
Page - 2 -
October 21, 1953

She was appointed by President Truman as United States representative to
Liberia, upon the inauguration of President Tubman, thus representing Daytona
Beach in West Africa.

She was largely influential in bringing the W.A.A.C. to Daytona Beach, and
in bringing the Men's army to this city.

Through her influence and representation, the first Low-cost Housing Project
was approved for Daytona Beach, and she influenced, largely, the bringing
of the second Housing Project to this city.

She brought such National figures as Vice-President Marshall of the United
States, Mrs. Eleanor Roosevelt and Governor Catts to Daytona Beach, as speak-
ers.

She brought Madame Pandit, Ambassador from India, now head of the United
Nations, to Daytona Beach.

She sponsored and directed an International conference of top-level women
of America and the World, on the campus of Bethune-Cookman College.

Mrs. Bethune cast the second vote for Women Suffrage in Daytona Beach,
giving the privilege of the first vote to Miss Cross because of her fight
for this cause.

She holds active membership in Stewart Memorial Methodist Church of Daytona
Beach, American Red Cross, Young Women's Christian Association and Fraternal
organizations. She is President of the Citizens Welfare League of this area.

Mrs. Bethune is seventy-eight years of age, a dynamic leader, a citizen of
which this community may well be proud.

CITIZEN'S WELFARE LEAGUE
EXECUTIVE COMMITTEE:

_____ Chairman

"IN UNITY THERE IS STRENGTH"

August 1, 1953

Judge Robert Wingfield
County Courthouse
Deland, Florida

Dear Judge Wingfield:

The Citizen's Welfare League of Daytona Beach would be very happy to have a conference with you at your convenience, someday when you are here in Daytona Beach. We are concerned about the things of our community, and we would like to discuss with you such matters as come under your jurisdiction.

We meet here at my house, 631 Pearl Street, Daytona Beach, if it is possible to give us an appointment when you can come to us, then we will arrange a meeting to discuss with you the matters we have in mind.

We hope this will not cause you to much inconvenience.

Sincerely yours,

Mary McLeod Bethune.

/gm

October 20, 1953

MARY McLEOD BETHUNE

1. Founded and built first school for higher learning in Daytona Beach.

2. Built and operated first hospital for Negroes for twenty years.

3. Brought the first water, light, and telephone lines from Ridgewood on west Second Avenue.

4. Organized the first Negro Ministerial Alliance in Daytona Beach.

5. Organized the first Civic Woman's Club among Negroes in Daytona Beach.

6. Organized and conducted the first Sunday afternoon Community Service in Daytona Beach, hence the organizing and building of Peabody Auditorium.

7. Administered the setting up of National Youth Administration in Daytona Beach, and the forty-eight states of the union.

8. Appointed by Franklin D. Roosevelt to serve as U. S. Consul in the setting up of the United Nations in San Francisco, thus representing Daytona Beach.

9. Appointed by President Truman as U. S. representative at the inauguration of President Tubman of Liberia, Africa, hence a representative of Daytona Beach.

10. Helped largely, to influence the comming of the W. A. A. C. to Daytona Beach.

11. Helped to influence the coming of the men's army to Daytona Beach.

12. Secured the first Housing Project and largely influenced the second for Daytona Beach.

13. Brought Vice-President Marshall of U. S. to Daytona Beach as speaker.

14. Brought Governor Catts of Florida to Daytona Beach, as speaker.

15. Brought Mrs. Roosevelt here as speaker on two occassions.

16. Brought Madame Pandit, Ambassador of India, now head of United Nations to Daytona Beach.

17. Held an international conference of top woman of America and world here two years ago.

18. Cast the second vote for woman sufferage in Daytona Beach, giving the first vote to Miss Cross, because of her fight for the cause.

19. Member – Church, Red Cross, Y. W. C. A., Elks, Eastern Star.

ADDRESS OFFICIAL COMMUNICATIONS TO
THE SECRETARY OF STATE
WASHINGTON 25, D. C.

**DEPARTMENT OF STATE**

WASHINGTON

January 2, 1952.

My dear Mrs. Bethune:

    It gives me pleasure to inform you that you have been designated a member of the United States Delegation to attend the inaugural ceremonies of His Excellency William V. S. Tubman as President of the Republic of Liberia, which are scheduled to take place at Monrovia from January 5 through January 14, 1952.

    Other members of the delegation, which is to be headed by Ambassador Edward R. Dudley, include Mr. Carl Murphy and Major General James S. Stowell, USAF.

    With best wishes for a successful mission,

                Sincerely yours,

                Dean Acheson

Mrs. Mary McLeod Bethune,
    Care of the Department of State,
        Washington, D. C.

*Sum*

*return to Mo. Bethune*

DEPARTMENT OF STATE
Washington, D. C.
November 30, 1951

Mrs. Mary McLeod Bethune,
1416 North Boulevard,
Tampa, Florida

Dear Mrs. Bethune:

The Government of the United States has been invited by the
Government of Liberia to send a delegation to the Inauguration of
its recently elected President, W. B. S. Tubman.  The Ceremony is to
take place in the Capital  City of Monrovia, January 5-14, 1952.

In view of the national traditionally close relationship with
the Republic of Liberia, the Department of State desires to send a
delegation representing those Americans who are interested in Liberia
and in American policies regarding Liberia and Africa.

Because of your long established interest in Liberia and of the
high regard with which you are viewed by the Liberian Government, the
President has suggested that I invite you to serve as a member of the
United States Delegation to the Inauguration. It is our hope that the
delegation will consist of Ambassador Edward R. Dudley as Chief of
the delegation, Robert M. Hutchins of the Ford Foundation, Carl Murphy
of the Afro-American of Baltimore, and you.

Travel to and from Liberia will be accomplished by air. [All
transportation expense will be borne by the Department of State.
There will be a per diem of $20.00 while in transit and during your
stay in Monrovia.] Housing in Monrovia will be provided in the
American Compound.

I sincerely hope you will be able to undertake this mission.
I will appreciate having an answer as soon as possible.

Sincerely,
George C. McGhee,
ASSISTANT SECRETARY OF STATE

CONSULATE-GENERAL
OF THE
REPUBLIC OF LIBERIA
220 BROADWAY
NEW YORK 38, N. Y.

*File*

12 April 1954

Dear Dr. Bethune:

    Upon the completion of my tour, visiting Liberian students in the United States, and return to New York, I wish to express grateful appreciation of the courtesy and cordiality as well as the kindness and hospitality shown us during our visit to your institution.

    It was a great pleasure to observe the operation of your great institution.

    You have my sincere congratulations on the splendid work you are performing, and best wishes for your continued success and prosperity.

    I wish to state also that I am grateful to you for the kind attention that is being given to the Liberian students who are enrolled at your institution. Their scholastic activities are indeed gratifying.

    Mrs. Yancy joins me in kindest regards and best wishes.

               Very truly yours,

               Ernest J. Yancy
    SECRETARY OF PUBLIC INSTRUCTION OF LIBERIA

Dr. Mary McCloud Bethune
    Bethune-Cookman College
    Daytona Beach, Florida

STATE OF FLORIDA )
COUNTY OF VOLUSIA )

BE IT KNOWN that before me, P. W. Harvey, a notary public in and
for the State of Florida at Large, and in the presence of the
witnesses hereinafter named and undersigned, personally came and
appeared ALBERT McLEOD BETHUNE, of full age, and voluntarily without any coercion and of his own free will made the following affi-
davit and acknowledgment in compliance with 731.29 Florida Statu-
tes Annotated: That he is a resident of Daytona Beach, Florida.
That he is the father of a certain male child, to-wit: one named
and called by the name of Albert E. Bethune who was born on November 14, 1921 at Miami, Dade County, Florida, and whose mother
was Meeba Mohl; that the said male child was afterwards, at
Baltimore, Maryland, duly adopted by Mary McLeod Bethune, the
mother of affiant, and said male child was thereafter known as
Albert McLeod Bethune, Jr., and thereafter said child lived with
and was supported by affiant, and said male child is now a member
of the armed forces, serial No. 14174092; that the said affiant,
Albert McLeod Bethune, further acknowledged before me that it was
his desire to recognize said male child, Albert McLeod Bethune, Jr.,
as his own child and capable of inheriting affiant's estate, real
and personal, as if born in wedlock.

IN WITNESS WHEREOF, I, ALBERT McLEOD BETHUNE, have hereunto set
my hand and seal this 10th day of April, A. D. 1945.

Attested by us as witnesses      *Albert McLeod Bethune*

Given under my hand and official seal at Daytona Beach, said
County and State this 10th day of April, A. D. 1945.

                 *P. W. Harvey*
                 Notary Public, State of Florida
                 My commission expires Nov. 21, 1945

*Reits 0436*

BIOGRAPHICAL SKETCH

MARY McLEOD BETHUNE

DATE OF BIRTH: JULY 10, 1875

PLACE OF BIRTH: Mayesville, South Carolina

DATE OF DEATH: May 18, 1955

PARENTS: Samuel McLeod and Patsy McIntosh McLeod

Married Albertus Bethune, May, 1898; one son, Albert McLeod Bethune, Sr.; two grand-children, Albert McLeod Bethune, II and Evelyn Idell Bethune; six great-grandchildren, Donald McLeod Bethune, Albert McLeod Bethune, III, Samuel McLeod Bethune, Patricia Antionette Bethune, Michael Mohl Bethune, and Mary Elizabeth Bethune.

EDUCATION: Country school, Mayesville, South Carolina; Scotia Seminary, Concord, North Carolina, graduated 1893; Moody Bible Institute, Chicago, Illinois, 1893-95.

HONORARY DEGREES:    A.M. - Wilberforce University, Wilberforce, Ohio, 1915
           M.S. - South Carolina State College, Orangeburg, South Carolina
           L.L.D.- Lincoln University, Philadelphia, Pennsylvania, 1935
           L.L.D.- Howard University, Washington, D. C., 1942
           L.L.D.- Atlanta University, Atlanta, Georgia, 1945
           L.L.D.- Wiley College, Marshall, Texas, 1943
           M.S.   - Tuskegee Institute, Alabama, 1938
           Doctor of Humanities - Bennett College, Greensboro, North
                                  Carolina, 1945
           Doctor of Humanities - West Virginia State College, Institute,
                                  West Virginia, 1947
           Doctor of Humanities - Rollins College, Winter Park, Florida, 1949.
                                  (Awarded for the first time to a person of
                                  color by a Southern white institution.)

EXPERIENCE: Instructor, Haines Institute, Augusta, Georgia, 1895 - 1896
           Instructor, Palatka Mission School, Palatka, Florida, 1899 - 1903
           Founded Daytona Normal and Industrial School for Negro Girls, 1904 (Now Bethune-Cookman College)
           President, Bethune-Cookman College, 1904 - 1942
           Director, Negro Affairs, National Youth Administration, 1936 - 1944
           Special Advisor to President Franklin D. Roosevelt on Minority Affairs,
                                               1936-44
           Special Assistant to Secretary of War for Selection of Candidates for first Officers' Cnadidates School for WACS, 1942

AFFILIATIONS:   President, Advisory Board, Bethune-Cookman College, 1954-55
           One of Founders and Past-President, Central Life Insurance Company
           Past-President, Florida State Teachers Association
           Founder, President-Emeritus, National Association of Colored Women
           Past-President, U. S. Branch - The United Peoples of Africa
           Past-President, Florida State Federation of Colored Women's Clubs

STATE BOARD OF HEALTH
BUREAU OF VITAL STATISTICS

**CERTIFICATE OF LIVE BIRTH**

FLORIDA JUN 1952

BIRTH NO. 109- 52-025948

REGISTRAR'S NO. 340

| 1. PLACE OF BIRTH | | | 2. USUAL RESIDENCE OF MOTHER (Where does mother live?) | | |
|---|---|---|---|---|---|
| a. COUNTY Volusia | | | a. STATE Florida | b. COUNTY Volusia | |
| b. CITY (If outside corporate limits, write RURAL) OR TOWN Daytona Beach | CODE NO. 74-11 | | c. CITY (If outside corporate limits, write RURAL) OR TOWN Daytona Beach | | |
| c. FULL NAME OF HOSPITAL OR INSTITUTION (If NOT in hospital or institution, give street address or location) Halifax District Hospital | | | d. STREET ADDRESS (If rural, give location) 618 Cypress St. | | |

| 3. CHILD'S NAME (Type or print) | a. (First) Evelyn | b. (Middle) Idell | c. (Last) Bethune |
|---|---|---|---|

| 4. SEX Female | 5a. THIS BIRTH SINGLE ☒ TWIN ☐ TRIPLET ☐ | 5b. IF TWIN OR TRIPLET (This child born) 1ST ☐ 2ND ☐ 3RD ☐ | 6. DATE OF BIRTH (Month) (Day) (Year) April 14, 1952 |
|---|---|---|---|

**FATHER OF CHILD**

| 7. FULL NAME | a. (First) Albert | b. (Middle) McLeod | c. (Last) Bethune, Sr. | 8. COLOR OR RACE Negro |
|---|---|---|---|---|
| 9. AGE (At time of this birth) 52 YEARS | 10. BIRTHPLACE (State or foreign country) South Carolina | 11a. USUAL OCCUPATION Teacher | 11b. KIND OF BUSINESS OR INDUSTRY Bethune Cookman College | |

**MOTHER OF CHILD**

| 12. FULL MAIDEN NAME | a. (First) Elizabeth | b. (Middle) | c. (Last) Sterricks | 13. COLOR OR RACE Negro |
|---|---|---|---|---|
| 14. AGE (At time of this birth) 32 YEARS | 15. BIRTHPLACE (State or foreign country) Fla. | 16. CHILDREN PREVIOUSLY BORN TO THIS MOTHER (Do NOT include this child) | | |

| | | a. How many OTHER children are now living? 1 | b. How many OTHER children were born alive but are now dead? 0 | c. How many children were stillborn (born dead after 20 weeks pregnancy)? 0 |
|---|---|---|---|---|

| 17. INFORMANT | Albert R. Bethune Sr. |
|---|---|

I hereby certify that this child was born alive on the date stated above.

| 18a. SIGNATURE Stanford S. Setern M.D. | 18b. ATTENDANT AT BIRTH M.D. ☒ MIDWIFE ☐ OTHER (Specify) |
|---|---|
| 18c. ADDRESS Daytona Beach, Florida | 18d. DATE SIGNED April 30, 1952 |

| 19. DATE REC'D BY LOCAL REG. 5/1/52 | 20. REGISTRAR'S SIGNATURE Bonnie A. Mills Dep. | 21. DATE ON WHICH GIVEN NAME ADDED BY (Registrar) |
|---|---|---|

**CERTIFIED COPY**

I HEREBY CERTIFY THE ABOVE TO BE A TRUE AND CORRECT COPY OF THE ORIGINAL RECORD ON FILE IN THE BUREAU OF VITAL STATISTICS OF THE FLORIDA STATE BOARD OF HEALTH AT JACKSONVILLE, FLORIDA

(NOT VALID UNLESS THE SEAL OF THE FLORIDA STATE BOARD OF HEALTH IS AFFIXED)

Wilson T. Sowder, M.D.
STATE REGISTRAR

Everett H. Williams, Jr.
DIRECTOR, BUREAU OF VITAL STATISTICS

MAY 14 1958

*Mary McLeod Bethune*

*Scholarship Gala*

*Atlanta, GA*

*Friends and Family*

*Continue the Legacy*

Special thanks to archivist Kenneth Chandler of the National Parks Service and The National Archives for Black Women's History which holds many of the documents of the legacy of Mary McLeod Bethune. The archives collects materials about and illustrating Mary McLeod Bethune, the National Council of Negro Women, other African American women's organizations, and individuals associated with those organizations. The archives also documents the ongoing preservation and interpretation of the Bethune legacy. The archives collects information in all media with a special focus on the years of Mary McLeod Bethune's life, 1875-1955.

Kenneth J. Chandler, Archivist

Mary McLeod Bethune Council House NHS

National Archives for Black Women's History

1318 Vermont Avenue, NW

Washington, DC 20005-3607

202-673-2402 x240 (phone)

202-673-0014 (direct)

202-673-2415 (fax)

kenneth_chandler@nps.gov

# A M E N !